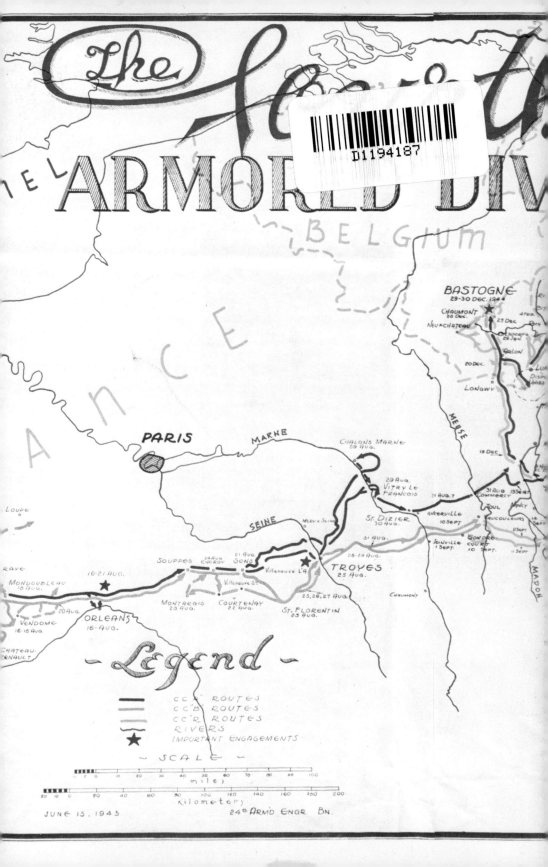

TIGER ★★ JACK

Major General John S. Wood

HANSON W. BALDWIN

★ ★

introduction by

Gen. Jacob L. Devers
USA, Retired

OLD ARMY PRESS

Library of Congress Catalog Card No. LC 78-61481
ISBN: 0-88342-059-7

Cover and Book Design by Leslie A. Johnston

PHOTO CREDITS:

Official U.S. Army photographs - pages 4, 29, 31 (bottom), 43, 90, 92, 93, 128, 166, 167.

Private photographs from the family of Gen. John S. Wood - pages 21, 27, 31 (top & middle), 35, 40, 46, 48, 72, 73, 77, 84, 87, 104, 107, 111, 114, 119, 121, 127, 152, 157.

THE OLD ARMY PRESS
1513 Welch
Ft. Collins, CO 80524

CONTENTS

The United States of America

honors the memory of

JOHN S. WOOD

This certificate is awarded by a grateful
nation in recognition of devoted and
selfless consecration to the service
of our country in the Armed Forces
of the United States.

Lyndon B. Johnson
President of the United States

ACKNOWLEDGMENTS

THIS BRIEF, INFORMAL MILITARY BIOGRAPHY IS BASED upon General Wood's unpublished memoirs, a 94 page manuscript written by him during his retirement entitled *Memories and Reflections*. I have quoted from this manuscript at length to allow the General to mirror himself in his own thoughts and phrases.

In addition to this memoir, I have drawn upon many of General Wood's papers, speeches and letters. Unless otherwise identified, the extensive quotations in the text are from General Wood's own memoirs or his other papers. My thanks are due to his family, who made these available. I have also utilized a biographical sketch of the General written by his son after his burial at West Point, and subsequently published in *Assembly* magazine, the quarterly publication of the U.S. Military Academy Association of Graduates, and in *Rolling Together,* a publication of the 4th Armored Division Association. Colonel John S. Wood, Jr. has made publication of *Tiger Jack* possible.

But even this brief study would not have been possible unless these sources had been heavily supplemented by official and unofficial histories, books, manuscripts, and reminiscences and recollections contributed by many of

Wood's friends and contemporaries and by 4th Armored Division records. Quotations are easily identified by sources in the context of the text; footnotes have been dispensed with in the interest of simplicity.

Of the published sources the following have been liberally drawn upon and frequently quoted:

The Fourth Armored Division, written and published by Captain Kenneth Koyen, Public Relations Officer, Fourth Armored Division. Munich, 1946.

Breakout and Pursuit, by Martin Blumenson. U.S. Army in World War II—The European Theatre of Operations. Office of the Chief of Military History, Dept. of the Army. Washington, 1961.

The Organization of Ground Combat Troops, by Kent Roberts Greenfield, Robert R. Palmer and Bell I. Wiley, of the Historical Section, Army Ground Forces. United States Army in World War II. Historical Division, Dept. of the Army. Washington, 1947.

The Lorraine Campaign, by H. M. Cole. U.S. Army in World War II—The European Theatre of Operations. Historical Division, Dept. of the Army. Washington, 1950.

Logistical Support of the Armies, Vol. I by Roland G. Ruppenthal. U.S. Army in World War II—The European Theatre of Operations. Office of the Chief of Military History, Department of the Army. Washington, 1953.

The Struggle for Europe, by Chester Wilmot. New York: Harper & Bros., 1952.

Patton—Ordeal and Triumph, by Ladislas Farago. New York: Obolensky, 1963.

Panzer Battles, by Major General F. W. von Mellenthin. Norman: University of Oklahoma Press, 1956.

The Infantry Journal, July, 1948. "Eggcup was the Call Sign," by Colonel Roger J. Browne.

What They Said About the Fourth Armored Division, compiled and published by the Public Relations Section, Headquarters, Fourth Armored Division.

Landshut, 1945.

The Nancy Bridgehead, prepared by subordinate commanders and staff of Combat Command A, 4th Armored Division (Lt. Col. Hal C. Pattison). Fort Knox, Ky.: The Armored School, 1947.

Manuscript sources that have been of considerable use and which are quoted where pertinent include the after action reports of the 4th Armored Division during the period of General Wood's command; "Summary of Operations of the 4th Armored Division in France, 17 July through 7 December 1944"; Combat History 4th Armored Division (for pertinent dates); and "The Operations of Combat Command A, 4th Armored Division; 28 July to 31 August, 1944," by Lieutenant Colonel Hal C. Pattison, Fort Leavenworth, Kansas: Command and General Staff College, 1946-47.

I am also indebted to Brigadier General Hal C. Pattison, U.S.A. (Ret.), former Director of Military History of the Army, for useful reminiscences, for reading and checking the manuscript, and for suggesting and identifying sources. My thanks also go to Mr. Martin Blumenson, distinguished historian.

In addition many other individuals contributed materially to this account; in fact, their enthusiastic responses were in themselves the finest kind of tribute to a fine soldier.

I am indebted to the following, most of whom are quoted in these pages, for letters and/or interviews:

General of the Army Dwight D. Eisenhower
Sir Basil Liddel Hart, *D. Litt.*
General Creighton W. Abrams, USA
Major General Archibald V. Arnold, USA (Ret.)
Major General Roger J. Browne, USAF (Ret.)
Mr. Robert L. Brown
General Bruce C. Clarke, USA (Ret.)
Lieutenant General Willis D. Crittenberger, USA (Ret.)
Major General Holmes E. Dager, USA (Ret.)
General Jacob L. Devers, USA (Ret.)
Lieutenant Colonel Risden L. Fountain
Lieutenant General Hobert R. Gay, USA (Ret.)

General Paul D. Harkins, USA (Ret.)
General W. M. Hoge, USA (Ret.)
Mr. Kenneth Koyen
Mr. George M. Mardikian
Major General C. L. Mullins, USA (Ret.)
Mr. Arthur P. Nesbit
Mr. Edward Rapp
Major General DeWitt C. Smith, Jr., USA
General Carl Spaatz, USAF (Ret.)
General O. P. Weyland, USAF (Ret.)

INTRODUCTION

"ALL HISTORY BECOMES SUBJECTIVE; IN OTHER WORDS, THERE IS PROPERLY NO HISTORY; ONLY BIOGRAPHY."
(EMERSON)

TO KNOW THE LIFE OF 'P' WOOD IS TO UNDERSTAND the history and the gallant prowess of the 4th Armored Division. He trusted his men, and they were true to him; he treated them greatly, and they showed themselves great.

A careful perusal of this slim volume is not merely to learn historic facts about a general who commanded an armored division in World War II. It is rather to recognize the wisdom of placing trust in one's fellowmen; it is to admire heartily the courage of a man who had a goal in mind and who consistently remained undaunted in the face of fearsome obstacles; it is to realize that compassion and humility, rather than harshness and egotistical pride, are the marks of strong character.

These are the timeless truths that make the story of 'P' Wood not just another account of a military figure of several decades ago. Here was a soldier—and we who fought with him were thankful he was a soldier and that he was on our side—but the things about him that made him a great soldier are the things that make a great human being. That is

13

why his story is a timeless one, one that will never be dated, outmoded, obsolete, even though wars among men may one day finally cease.

The story of General John Shirley Wood is exemplary for every person who wants to fulfill honorably a worthy destiny—whatever his chosen walk of life may be—exemplary for every person who yearns to fulfill nobly the role he knows to be his own role.

> 'P' Wood, himself trustworthy, placed trust in others;
>   confident that his cause was just, he went forward
>   fearlessly despite known and unknown obstacles;
>   compassionate where others were concerned, he was
>   humble where he himself was concerned—
>   in these attitudes lay his invincible strength.

Of my good friend and comrade-at-arms, 'P' Wood, can be truly said what every man would like to have said of himself and of the way he lived out his life among his fellow-man: "Well done!"

General Jacob L. Devers
U.S.A., Retired

14

★ 1 ★

THE LEADER AND THE LED

THE SHAPING OF A GENERAL, LIKE THE MAKING OF A
soldier, is a complex process involving both heredity and
environment, tradition and experience. It is a process that
defies precise definition or consistent pattern. Like the miracle
of man, it can be examined but never completely analyzed.

Good generals can be made by their own and others'
efforts, and poor generals, fortunately, rarely live in history.
Great generals, like great writers, poets, or artists, are born,
not made, yet the influences that touch their lives unquestionably shape their careers.

The role of division commander presents the supreme
test of generalship. The division, the standard tactical unit of
most armies (about 10,000 to 20,000 men), is normally the
largest outfit upon which any single man can fully impress
his personality and bestow his cachet of leadership, and the
smallest unit with the capability of sustained land combat.
The division commander is either the basic architect of
victory or the scapegoat of defeat, for the division is the
building-block of ground war. What the division commander
does, how his division performs, affects—and may, indeed,
determine—the fate, not only of the division itself, but of
the Corps and the Army.

At this level of command there is no place to hide. The inexorable demands of battle and the multiple responsibilities of high command will quickly reveal the deficiencies of the poor general, or will highlight the virtues of the good commander. Thus, it is not by accident that the great divisions of history have been known by the names of their commanders. The demanding responsibilities and technical know-how implicit in such a command winnow the grain from the chaff, for a division is the threshing machine of generalship. The division commander's job is, in short, the cornerstone—just as the division is the building block—of the whole tactical edifice of an army.

A division commander serves at a level where tactics leave off and strategy begins, where the art of how to win the battle blends into the art of how to win the war. The division also presents its commander with all the problems of the military art: leadership; knowledge of the enemy; planning; supply and administration; the coordination of all arms and weapons; mutual support; in short, the multiple problems of command. Indeed, the skills required, the professional knowledge needed, and the character and personality necessary to lead a division successfully in battle represent a combination of qualities rarely found in a single individual.

* * * * * * * *

"P" [Professor] Wood, whose name is indissolubly connected with that of the 4th Armored Division—"They shall be known by their deeds alone"—was a leader. He was a division commander little known to the public. But he has been called by Liddell Hart, the British military critic, "The Rommel of the American armored forces . . . one of the most dynamic commanders of armor in World War II," and General George Patton once said, "The accomplishments of this division have never been equalled."

"And by that statement," Patton added, "I do not mean this war (World War II), I mean in the history of warfare. There has never been such a superb fighting organization as the 4th Armored Division."

18

General Eisenhower described Wood as "a natural leader." The Germans called "P" Wood "Tiger Jack," and his men loved him. "They would follow him to hell today," General Jacob L. Devers said long after Wood had retired.

There was a warmth and magnetism about "P" Wood, an identification with his men, an emotional involvement in their lives and a great pride in them, which rubbed off on those he commanded. In his memoirs, Wood once enumerated the characteristics of combat leadership which he believed to be fundamental:

> First, there is the disregard of fear which passes for bravery; second, there is an unceasing endeavor to spare the men one has the honor to lead unnecessary hardships and useless losses; third, there is a willingness and desire to share their needed hardships and face their same dangers; fourth, there is the quality of sympathy and human understanding that inspires confidence and trust and willing effort and initiative among one's troops.

> To me Robert E. Lee embodied these qualities in the highest degree, and one can well understand the remark of a Confederate soldier when Lee appeared one day in the front lines of battle. Lee stood looking at his weary men, saying no word as they moved into combat; but one of them, choked with emotion, said:

> "I will fight all the way to hell itself, after what the General has just *said* to us."

Wood epitomized these qualities he described and, like Lee, he inspired affection.

*   *   *   *   *   *   *   *

This story of a general—some of it told in his own words—deals with the career, brief in combat, of a Division Commander, and with the 4th Armored Division, "P" Wood's pride and joy. General Wood was a fine division commander and the 4th Armored Divsion a great division in the days of its glory. The United States fielded some crack combat outfits in World War II, and produced men like Huebner,

Barton, Ryder, "Gravel-Voice" Harmon, Manton Eddy, and many others, to lead them, men whose names, unfortunately, are virtually unknown to today's generations. In every case the good divisions and their leaders were inseparable; the commanders and their men were linked forever in history by that indefinable intangible so many have tried to measure and define: leadership.

General Wood commanded his division in combat for only a little more than four months. But he had trained the 4th Armored for two years before the division won its military immortality in the Normandy breakout, and the stamp of his methods set the pattern for the division's performance under two other commanders throughout the remaining months—from December 1944, to May 1945, of World War II. The division won a Presidential unit citation, three Medals of Honor, and praise from the "GI's" themselves as "the best damn armored division in the European Theatre of war."

Much of the division's success was a reflection of its first commander's generalship and leadership. The 4th Armored Division was in large measure what "P" Wood made it. Like all men mortal he was not, of course, without faults and weaknesses. He had very definite opinions and expressed them—not always a politic trait in a military organization— and he did not hesitate to cut the corners of command and to ignore"the book." His outspoken criticisms of what he considered the misuse of armor by higher commanders possibly helped to end his combat career prematurely, but throughout World War II the 4th Armored Division bore the indelible mark of Wood's training, his tactical concepts, his methods of command, his mark of military greatness. Its finest accolade came from the enemy in a SHAEF intelligence report:

> The 4th Armored Division is both feared and hated by German front line troops because of its high combat efficiency . . . the . . . division has gained a reputation amongst the Wehrmacht of being a crack armored unit dangerous to oppose.

*   *   *   *   *   *   *   *

In the Normandy hedgerows, the ugly tanks were mustered in that hot July of 1944. They were a far cry, indeed, from the lumbering monsters that had lurched across the cratered battlefield at Cambrai in another war in the first great armored action of history. The tanks of the 4th Armored Division were chiefly Shermans (the General Sherman M-4), a medium tank, of about 35 tons, with a 75 mm. gun and a five man crew. The Sherman was an ugly vehicle, with a high silhouette—broiling in summer heat, frigid in winter cold. It was no match in gun power or armor for the German Tigers or Panthers, but it was the mainstay of U.S. armored forces, and, indeed, of the Allied armies, in World War II. It had a rubber-block track, with about five times the life of the steel tracks used by the enemy; its engine was powerful and sound and almost 50,000 of them were built throughout the war. Old Mr. Reliable was a far more mobile tank than those slow crawling monsters of Cambrai, and mobility was the 4th Armored Division's middle name. The Sherman's purpose was, nevertheless, the same as those tanks of an earlier war: to change the battle of static positions and fixed lines into a war of movement; to exploit a breakthrough; to

Sherman Tank - Thunderbolt V on the battlefield in France. Lt. Col. C.W. Abrams command tank (37th Tank Battalion) and crew. (Abrams later became Chief of Staff, U.S. Army).

get the battle moving; to turn against the enemy his own tactics of Blitzkrieg.

The U.S. armored divisions of World War II were, organizationally, ahead of their time; they set the tactical style — task forces, building blocks, combat commands that could be tailored to any task — that now dominates the army of today.

The armored division, at the time of Normandy, was a lean, flexible outfit of almost 11,000 men, and 263 tanks, including Shermans, and light tanks (a 16 ton tank with a four-man crew and a 37 mm. gun). Its infantry strength had been increased as a result of our early experiences in Africa; its tank strength had been reduced. The 4th had three armored infantry battalions, transported in half-track vehicles (front steering wheels and tracks in the rear), totalling about 3,000 men. The tanks of the Division were organized in three tank battalions, each designed to operate in "married" team formations, with the infantry battalions. The Division's artillery consisted of three battalions, armed with 54, 105 mm., self-propelled howitzers to provide artillery support; a cavalry reconnaissance squadron (with jeeps, armored cars and light tanks); and an engineer battalion with some bridging equipment. Maintenance, medical, and other units provided the indispensable back-up to the combat units. A number of attached units augmented the strength and fire power of the division, including a tank destroyer battalion, self-propelled high-velocity 76 mm. guns, and a self-propelled antiaircraft artillery battalion. The division was organized in two combat commands, "A" and "B", and a reserve command, the whole unit was keyed to mass-times-momentum — to smashing power and to speed, to ramble and to roll.

The 4th Armored was new to war — new, too, to the Army list — but it traced its spiritual continuity, its heritage, its tradition, back to the days of the "Yellowlegs" and the horse artillery, back to Pelham's guns and the "foot cavalry" of other battles, other times, whose prodigies of mobility had made military history . . .

The basic hallmarks of the division . . . were rapid flanking movement, deep penetration and constant momentum; all coupled with violent execution of fire and maneuver . . .

★ 2 ★

THE DIVISION
Deep Penetration

THE GENERAL
The Beginnings:
Birth and Heritage

★ THE DIVISION ★

IN JULY 1944, U.S. AND BRITISH ARMIES HAD SUCCESS-
fully established a foothold in "Festung Europa," had broken
through the shoreline crust of the Westwall, and had won a
firmly held beachhead in Normandy. But the difficult hedgerow country and a tenacious German defense had contained
the Allied forces. Once again, as in the trench stalemate of
World War I, the armies were locked in a bitter struggle of
static positions.

The 4th Armored had not landed in France until D
plus 36—36 days after the invasion of June 6—after a cross-
Channel trip from England. During its brief stay in the apple
orchards and shell-damaged towns of the Contentin Peninsula,
the Division had been busy checking its equipment: its tanks,
its "peeps" (jeeps), its armored cars and trucks and self-
propelled guns—the vehicles that were part of the table of
equipment of a U.S. armored division. The division's armored
infantry battalions briefly took over a section of the static
front near Carentan, relieving the weary 4th Infantry Division.

Major General John Shirley Wood, the division commander, "went down to look the situation over and stopped
by Bradley's headquarters on the way." (General Omar N.
Bradley, commanding the U.S. First Army, and later the U.S.

12th Army Group).

I found Bradley and my classmate Johnny Walker
[Major General Walton H. Walker, later commander
of the U.S. Eighth Army in Korea] in a trailer and
told them I was ready to move but hoped we were
not to be kept long in a static defense role as we had
only a relatively small infantry component and I
hated to lose my armored infantry who had been
trained to operate with tanks on the move. It was
then that Bradley remarked that it had been necessary
to "blood"* newly arriving units to prove their
mettle. This remark disgusted and infuriated me and I
so expressed myself in no uncertain terms, saying that
my people would do whatever they had to do without the need of any blood-bath. I knew my division,
and its soldiers never failed me, although our infantry
casualties in that dismal hedgerow combat were
numerous and painful.

When Operation COBRA—the breakout—smashed the
German lines, the tanks and jeeps of the 4th Armored galloped
through the gap and drove relentlessly toward the base of
the Cherbourg peninsula, the gateway to Brittany and the
pivot to the whole German position in Normandy. The 4th
Armored spearheaded the main effort of the VIII Corps, and,
indeed, of all the U.S. ground forces.

The division rumbled through the break in the German
lines at 0945 on 28 July, passed through two U.S. infantry
divisions, and, despite German roadblocks, mines, and

---

*Throughout his life Wood disliked the term "blooded,"
used by so many military leaders. He felt not only that it was
a de-humanizing term, but the process of deliberately exposing
green troops to combat and casualties was unnecessary as
part of a training program if a division had been properly
trained. Other good soldiers and some expert observers, like
Martin Blumenson, disagreed, however, and some believed
that the few days the 4th Armored spent in static positions
near Carentan steadied and schooled it for what was to come.

Normandy, 1944, Maj. Gen. Wood confers with Lt. Gen. Bradley, CG 1st US Army, just before the breakthrough in August 1944.

Coutances, France, 1944. 4th Armored Infantry cleaning out.

sporadic resistance, it crunched to Coutances, 18 miles behind the broken front. Behind it were by-passed strong points, dazed and wandering enemy, scattered units—some still fighting cohesively and well. The latter were to be left to the mop-up forces; the key to the 4th's tactics was *movement.*

The 4th was commanded by a *commanding* General; Wood led the fight wherever he was and he was all over the place. He was "no rear-area commander. He kept well forward, knowing that armored actions and enemy reaction happen fast in combat. He said: 'If you can't *see* it happen, it's too late to hear about it back in a rear area and meet it with proper force'."

27

At Coutances, he came up to the Command Post of CC B (Combat Command B), Brigadier General Holmes E. Dager, commanding, in a "depression in the road about 200 yards behind the front lines. As Wood arrived he was welcomed by a heavy shower of German mortar fire. He and Dager dove head-first into the ditch beside the road and *face*-first into a mass of thistles. Wood solemnly remarked: 'You pick some damned prickly spots for your CP's'."

It was near Countances that Wood demonstrated the sang-froid, courage, and calmness that earned him the Distinguished Service Cross. The youngest officer in the division, a rifle platoon commander who had been one of Wood's tennis competitors during the months in England, recalls his astonishment at seeing General Wood by the side of the road:

> We were under increasingly intense small arms fire, a tank and a jeep had been knocked out by AT mines, and things were somewhat uncertain and disorganized.
>
> General Wood spotted me, said, "Smith, it doesn't look like we'll get in much tennis today," and then proceeded to walk down the road with me, his arm around my shoulder for an instant. In the next few moments, oblivious to the firing, he put the situation in perspective for me in a father-to-son discussion, oriented me, and then sent me on my way—ready to attack anything anywhere, and with a better idea of how to do it . . . .
>
> . . . [Later, the general] , clad immaculately, as always, in polished boots, riding pants, a trim jacket and sun glasses, which he wears rain or shine . . . marched into the town on foot under fire, captured a German soldier . . . found a path through the minefields, picked his way through the town on foot, sending back a message for his troops to follow him.

The message, which has become a classic phrase in the history of the "tankers" was simple:

General Dager, send the infantry through after me.

Coutances, France. Gen. Wood interrogating German soldier on location of mines. Wood took the soldier prisoner bare handed and was later handed his pistol by his driver.

Self-propelled howitzer of Battery B, 22nd Armored Field Artillery Battalion moving through Coutances, France.

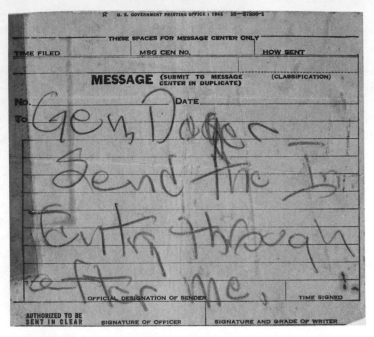

Coutances, France, July 19, 1944. The classic message Maj. Gen. Wood sent to Brig. Gen. Dager . . .

". . . using any road," by General Wood's orders, the division moved rapidly on Avranches, by-passing German strong points and ignoring scattered enemy units. One column almost overran (it missed by several hundred yards) the advanced command post of the German Seventh Army, and narrowly missed capturing General Paul Hausser, the commander, and several of his staff. The high-ranking German brass fled on foot, and then by vehicle, to the east.

In the French countryside the division left a comet's tail of prisoners marching with the dazed and crumbled look of the defeated, but the look seemed lighted guardedly from within by the wonder of surviving. By the time the division reached Avranches, fifty miles from its former lines, the prisoner bag had risen to 3,000. The tanks, tank destroyers, and peeps were still moving forward over the dusty roads. As they advanced the French tricolors went up in the villages, the Resistance herded collaborators into the squares, and the people shouted — there was a general air of jubilee everywhere.

But this was not merely a campaign of madder music and stronger wine; there were short, sharp, fire fights, sudden

Vannes, Brittany, 1944. Townspeople welcome 4th Armored tanks rumbling through the main street (notice effigy of Hitler's head over guillotine basket).

Avranches, France. German POW's taken by 4th Armored Division.

Avranches, France, July 31, 1944. 4th Armored tanks seize the communications gateway to France.

forays, and forever the unending crunch across the roads and fields of France. In five days the 4th left behind in its furrowed wake the ruck and remnants of three enemy infantry divisions, a paratrooper division, and some shattered tanks of the 2nd SS Panzer Division.

By 31 July, the 8th Tank Battalion of the 4th Armored was bivouacked and laagered up, miles behind the crumbling German lines in Normandy near Avranches, the communications gateway to all of France. Behind them German units were scattered like a flock of squawking chickens, on flanks and in the rear; ahead of them lay the wide open spaces.

Sergeant C. A. Klinga, C Company, 8th Tank Battalion, coined a battle cry at Avranches that was to live throughout the war:

They've got us surrounded again, the poor bastards.

Sergeant Klinga was right. The "poor bastards" didn't know what had hit them.

By the end of July the German situation in France had become, in German words, "one hell of a mess" (*Riesensauerei*). The German "defenses in the Cotentin had crumbled and disintegrated" and the Americans "controlled the last natural defensive line before Brittany." In the words of the U.S. Army Official History,

> ...the sensational success of General Wood's 4th Armored Division had exploded the nightmare of static warfare that had haunted the Americans so long in the Cotentin.
>
> Under General Wood ... the style of fighting was set in this, the first of the division's many breakthrough operations. It was a daring, hard-riding, fastshooting style. The division's front was as wide as the road down which it sped. The recon men out front kept going until they hit resistance too hot to handle. Teams of tanks and armored infantrymen swung out smoothly in attack formation under the protective fire of the quickly emplaced artillery. The division broke the enemy or flowed about them, cutting the German lines of communication and splitting apart the units.

32

★ THE GENERAL ★

"P" WOOD WAS 56 YEARS OLD WHEN HE LED THE 4TH
Armored out of the Normandy hedgerows; for this moment
he had lived a lifetime.

Wood was born in a world where the gasoline engine—
dominant in the defeat of Germany—was little known.
Horse-cars and mule-cars and phaetons were familiar to his
youth; in later years he recalled the "ice-wagon horses,"
with their "straw hats through which their ears protruded
like wings, and . . . the magnificent brewery-wagon teams of
matched Percherons or Clydesdales . . . ."

Wood's father was Carroll D. Wood, an Arkansas circuit
judge who made his circuit of the brick county courthouses
in a "mule-drawn buckboard." Judge Wood later served for
34 years as Associate Justice of the Supreme Court of
Arkansas. His forebears were Scotch-Irish-English stock,
with quiet pride but no pretensions, schooled in the ancient
virtues and the homely philosophy which then so largely
characterized the American scene. Wood's was an unsophisti-
cated development, deeply influenced by parents he loved, in
an environment simple in values, technology and social
mores. His parents were God-fearing, upright people—not
worldly in the modern sense of the word, but cultivated.

Jack Wood learned the classics at his mother's knee, and he had read most of Dickens at a time when other southern children of his age were still on "Bre'r Rabbit."

The young Wood was a bright lad—strong, big, tough. He entered the University of Arkansas as a sophomore at 16, graduated with a degree in chemistry in three years, and was captain of the football team in his senior year. He was an energetic youth, with the large frame, the soft tread, and the seeming awkwardness but natural grace of the big athlete. He had a keen sense of homespun humor, and studies and sports did not siphon off enough of his ebullience to keep him entirely clear of trouble. During his junior year he conducted, as he put it, "certain laboratory experiments which led to a series of minor explosions on the steps of the women's library." The explosion resulted in his suspension from the University for part of his junior year. Later he wrote:

> During this time I worked as a tram man in a gold mine of the Silverton district in Colorado and saved enough to enter Stanford University in the fall of 1905. A combination of depleted funds, the earthquake [the famous San Francisco quake of 1906], and forgiveness from my own state university which needed a quarterback, brought me back home to complete my courses.

Already, as an undergraduate, Wood had demonstrated some of the qualities of leadership, both on the athletic field and on the campus. He showed, too, an independence of mind and action which was later to characterize his military career. During this period he

> ...heartily disliked any implication of military discipline and had postponed the "drill" requirement for graduation until my senior year in college, when I made it up by enrolling in the university band to learn the clarinet—an instrument which I have always detested.

After graduation from the University of Arkansas in 1907 he took a job as instructor in chemistry at the University,

Univeristy of Arkansas, 1907. Young Wood in football garb. He captained the team his senior year and played tackle and end.

and assistant state chemist, at what seemed to him the munificent salary of $85 a month plus food.

Wood's early and formative life gave little promise of future military greatness. He disliked, as he said, military discipline, and a career in chemistry seemed foreordained. But he had demonstrated an inquiring and curious mind, a quickness to assimilate knowledge, and the leadership qualities of a natural athlete.

Perhaps even more important, man and the moment had met. Young Robert Hyatt, Wood's roommate and teammate at the University of Arkansas, had obtained a West Point appointment, and he induced Wood to apply for one also. A "desire to play another year or so of football" influenced the young man favorably. Wood was appointed to West Point, reporting for the entrance examinations on a snowy day in 1908, in an era of burgeoning science and expanding industry. The Wright Brothers had just demonstrated powered flight; the horseless carriage was commencing to challenge old Dobbin; and, above all, the beginnings of the internal combustion engine and of electronics had heralded the start of an immense Technological Revolution—still unfinished sixty years later. These developments meant, inevitably, profound changes in the military art and an unstable period in world history. What Toynbee has described as a "time of troubles" was beginning, a time which was to lead to the greatest wars in the history of man.

Thus, natural ability and inherited characteristics, plus developed talents, circumstance, and just plain luck, all played a role in fashioning a military career.

★ 3 ★

THE DIVISION
Constant Momentum

THE GENERAL
The Long Gray Line

★ THE DIVISION ★

AT NOON, 1 AUGUST, 1944 AS THE 4TH ARMORED DIVI-
sion's tanks rumbled into Brittany, the United States Third
Army, General George Patton commanding, became operational. Patton and General Wood were close, perhaps as close
as Army commander and division commander could ever
become. They were both products of the Old Army, the
Army of horses and caissons rolling along; they were both
bred in the "l'audace, l'audace, toujours l'audace" school;
they were both students of military history.

Thus, it was fortunate, both for Wood and for history,
that the VIII Corps, with the 4th Armored as one of its
subordinate units, shifted from U.S. First, to U.S. Third
Army after the breakout. For both Patton and Wood were
tankers, schooled to speed and mobility and power; each
understood the other.

General Wood was the kind of division commander who
not only accepted responsibility but demanded it; the 4th
Armored was trained to move and keep moving. Wood
needed only a lightly checked rein, and from Patton he got
it.

Patton expected his division commanders to "exercise
independent judgment and tactical daring"; he granted them

France, 1944. Wood and Patton at the front - the 4th Armored was Patton's "Advance Guard".

a "freedom of action that permitted [them] . . . to be virtually independent . . . ."

This suited the 4th Armored to a **T**; the division, encouraged by its commander, took the bit in its teeth, and soon, as the Army's official history puts it, a naturally "headstrong crew became rambunctious in Brittany."

This division, and the Army in which it served, ignored the formalism of ordered warfare so dear to the heart of the linear theorists and to those impressed by the stalemate of World War I. Its tactics were organized chaos: a deliberate attempt to push and penetrate deeper into German rear areas, by-passing strong points, lapping around them and isolating them as the incoming tide laps around a tongue of sand. To get bogged down was the greatest crime; no outfit that kept moving could go far wrong in the 4th Armored.

The division command post changed position six times between 30 July and 10 August. Wood slept in a tent when he slept at all, and commanded from a jeep or a Piper cub flying over his forward elements. He gave oral orders and held tailgate conferences—not for him the formal briefings, the long written orders. His directives were always terse and simple; in effect, "Go get 'em." In later years Major General Holmes Dager recalled:

Wood hit fast, and hard!

A German General, surprised, overrun and captured with his staff by a 4th Armored column, remarked: "I would like to meet that General who commands 4th Armored Division—he is outstanding among Generals of American divisions."

Preparing an Army Corps attack-order, distributing it to the divisions and putting it out to lower units takes a little time. Wood's idea was action *now!* He used a system to get his orders out quickly, and start his attack rapidly. He used no ground transportation, but flew in his liaison plane to Corps Headquarters, listened to the Third Army and Corps plans, spoke briefly to Corps and other Division commanders about their parts in the Plan, scratched a few boundaries, objectives, and notes on a map he pulled out of his shirt, and took off again in his cub plane with a red streamer flying from the tip of each wing.

To assist General Wood in locating them, Combat Commanders Colonel Bruce Clarke (CC A) and Brigadier General Holmes Dager (CC B) marked their command tanks, usually with a French window-shade marked with an "A" or "B." When Wood flew over they exposed their marker and watched where he landed, usually in a field or on a road. There they met him.

"P" would pull the map out of his shirt, spread it and point . . . "here's your boundaries, the units left, right and following us and the first, second and third objectives—let's get·at it right now!" It was necessary to get him to lift his ham-size fist off the map to spot a village or terrain feature identifying the objectives. After brief details of enemy information, air and artillery support, Wood flew to the other Combat Commands, artillery headquarters, and to his division headquarters to brief his staff and put his concise attack order on a map and a few message-blanks.

By the time the Army Corps order arrived at Wood's headquarters at least one, and sometimes all the 4th Armored objectives had been taken and Combat Commands were mopping up and rolling over German forces previously knocked down. Wood's orders followed Patton's warning: "When you knock these ———— Krauts down, roll over them, *or* they'll get up and hurt you."

The rapid advance of the 4th Armored produced strange encounters. En route to Lorient, Combat Commands A and B wiped out one of the last vestiges of bygone wars: a division of horse cavalry, mounted Russian defectors and mercenaries, the 281st Ost Cavalry Battalion.

It was all movement in the campaign through Brittany — fire and movement, but mostly movement. The weather was hot, the days sunny; the roads of France spewed dust as the tank tracks churned and the Allied fighter-bombers soared above the armored columns.

In Brittany, it was "Boche kaput!" and wine, cider, eggs and kisses, with the tanks rolling, the enemy fleeing, the sharp scent of danger to heighten the intoxication of triumph, and interludes of short, bitter, fire fights with momentum briefly checked, before the tanks crunched forward again over the roads of France.

The tanks of the 4th Armored rolled over Rennes, which was strongly held, left its reduction to the following infantry, and kept moving.

But the division was checked by plans, conceived in caution before the invasion, perpetuated after the invasion by strategical inflexibility. The plan called for the capture of the Brittany ports as supply bases for the Allied armies. There were heavily garrisoned German fortresses at St. Nazaire, Lorient and Brest, and the "scenario" of invasion had anticipated a slow and orderly German retreat across France, vicious battles south of the Seine, and a requirement for the Brittany ports as bases of supply. The breakout at

Avranches, July 31, 1944. 4th Armored Division medium tank rumbles past knocked out light tank.

Avranches, France. 4th Armored Sherman knocked out in the attack on Avranches.

Avranches, however, changed all this. The Germans were obviously fleeing in disarray, and the mobility and shock effect of armored divisions would be wasted in attacking fortresses. The armor would be bogged down in street fighting against heavy defenses.

Wood saw all this sooner than most of his superiors. Even before Rennes was captured,

> General Wood conceived a spectacular idea. It already seemed evident to him [by 2 August] that the main action in Western Europe would take place not in Brittany but in central France. Few enemy forces remained in Brittany, so why proceed westward to the Atlantic ocean and a dead end . . .?

Instead of turning westwards towards Quiberon Bay, St. Nazaire and the Brittany ports, Wood sent part of his division southeast around Rennes, towards Chateaubriant and Angers. General Paul Harkins later recalled:

> When General Patton found out about this, he exploded. However, when he confronted "P" Wood about disobeying orders, "P" politely informed him the war was not going to be won by going West; the enemy was to the east. It didn't take General Patton long to see that "P" Wood was right.

Wood recorded in his memoirs that,

> . . . when I finally saw George Patton at Laval, George said, "You nearly got tried for that." To which I replied that someone should have been tried but it certainly was not I."

But it took time—too much time to General Wood's impatient mind—to persuade the high command to reorient the "schwerpunkt," or main effort, of the entire division. Referring to the Allied command, he told Major General Troy Middleton, his corps commander, ". . . [they] are winning the war the wrong way!"

B. H. Liddell Hart, the British military critic and historian, agreed with Wood. In his *History of the Royal Tank Regiment — The Tanks,* he wrote:

This wide open opportunity [the drive to the east from Angers] might have been exploited much earlier. General Wood, who led the breakout at Avranches, reached Rennes early on 2 August. While awaiting further orders, he took the initiative of thrusting a spearhead southeast to Angers on the Loire, ready to advance east. But on the 4th orders came that he must drive southwest from Rennes to Vannes, to cut off the Brittany peninsula. He protested strenuously, feeling sure that he could reach Chartres in two days, but had to comply with the decision of the High Command, who adhered to the COSSAC [Overlord] plan of trying to secure the west coast ports as a first stop. Even Patton seems to have lost the longer view in his eagerness to capture Brest [which actually held out under Ramke, until 19 September — 44 days after Patton triumphantly reported its capture].

Bruce Clarke supports Hart's analysis. Long after the war he wrote:

> Brest is a port where the water in the harbor rises and falls several feet with the . . . tide. Because of this the ships were "locked" into the harbor . . . . This required lock gates at the entrance . . . . Before we took Brest the Germans blew up these gates. This made Brest unuseable. All the wasted time in taking Brest was to no avail. Brest was never used by the Navy . . . . Hence, the Brest peninsula campaign cost us time, casualties and wasted effort when we should have been going East as "P" Wood wanted to do.

Some of the 4th's units had reached the outskirts of Lorient by 7 August, and Wood champed at the bit, hoping to be allowed to rampage to the east, into the heart of France.

The 4th was not long restrained; they were "Georgie's boys." Responsibility for the containment of Lorient was turned over to another division in mid-August, and the 4th Armored headed east, "constant momentum" still its motto.

During the first two weeks in August, the 4th Armored Division had displayed a constant and consistent aggressiveness. It had performed like cavalry — slashing, side-slipping and pushing forward. It had effectively exploited a fluid situation by using speed and surprise. Having made a reputation in the Cotentin, the division expanded it in Brittany. During the first twelve days of August, the 4th Armored Division took almost 5,000 prisoners and destroyed or captured almost 250 German vehicles. Against these figures, the division lost 98 killed, 362 wounded, 11 missing; 15 tanks and 20 vehicles ... The 4th Armored Division had developed to a high degree of proficiency a reckless ardor for pursuit of a defeated enemy. The esprit de corps of the troops matched the supreme confidence of the division commander....

Column of German prisoners of war taken by 4th Armored Division during action at Avranches.

★ THE GENERAL ★

A DESIRE TO PLAY MORE FOOTBALL BROUGHT JOHN Shirley Wood to West Point and his football reputation at the University of Arkansas got him in. He passed the scholastic entrance examinations with ease, but was told, "while standing naked on the scales in the Post Hospital," that he could not enter West Point because of an eye defect—myopia.

> At that moment Colonel Gandy, the head of the hospital and a football fan, came by and asked me if I had ever played football. When I said that I had been quarterback and captain of a college team in the Southwest, he said West Point needed a quarterback. I then told him that I was to be rejected on account of my eyes, and he immediately said he would see that the defect be waived. So, there I was, on the threshhold of nearly forty years' service in the Army, when I had expected to enter an academic career as a physical chemist.

Football brought Wood to West Point, but West Point, in its "subtle and unique way . . . left [Wood] forever under its spell and stamp." In his four years as a cadet he became— part and parcel, blood and bone, heart and spirit of the Long

Cadet Corporal Wood as a second classman (sophomore) at West Point.

Gray Line—forever tied to the Army.

He was a somewhat raunchy and unusual cadet: a college graduate who had earned his own living, older than many of his classmates, he considered himself much more sophisticated, even "blase," and he was certainly much more confident. He was, a classmate remembers,

> . . . a big lovable guy, with marvelous physique, fine mind, great confidence, an extrovert, a swashbuckler.
>
> As an athlete, he was impressive. He played a fine game in football as an end, in spite of a pinched nerve in his neck . . . . His fine bass voice made our Hundredth Night [an annual West Point jollity 100 nights before graduation] notable by his singing "Coleur de Rose," his theme song.

Wood entered West Point in 1908 and graduated in 1912—years when the U.S. Military Academy was the incubator for most of the military greats and near-greats who came to fame thirty years later in World War II. As a cadet Wood knew, and was known, to them all:

> Dwight D. Eisenhower, class of 1915, later General of the Army and Supreme Commander Allied Powers, President of the United States.
>
> Omar N. Bradley, Class of 1915, later General of the Army and Commander of the 12th Army Group and Chairman of the Joint Chiefs of Staff.
>
> General Carl ("Touhey") Spaatz, Class of 1914, later Commander of the Eighth Air Force.
>
> General Jacob L. Devers, Class of 1909, later Commander of the Sixth Army Group.
>
> General George S. Patton Jr., Class of 1909, later Commander of the Third Army.
>
> Robert L. Eichelberger, Class of 1909, later Commander of the U.S. Eighth Army.
>
> William H. Simpson, Class of 1909, later Commander of the U.S. Ninth Army.
>
> And a host of others.

The hazing of plebes by upperclassmen with the ostensible purpose of securing proper military posture and the early indoctrination of new cadets as to their status in the Corps was relatively unrestrained in my day, although it had been forbidden by an Act of Congress in 1901. There was no written Code of Conduct for new cadets such as that contained today in the official booklet, *The Fourth Class System.* But there was a well understood set of rules, customs, and traditions, which had accumulated in the century since the founding of the Military Academy, to which the plebe was supposed to conform under the gentle guidance and tender mercies of upper classmen.

The yearlings were naturally the most zealous and obnoxious in their insistence on conformity to the requirements from which they had emerged. I was older than most of these yearlings when I entered West Point and had finished college and worked for a living and their antics, particularly the members of the runt [cadets short in stature] companies, at first offended me. But when I realized it was all part of the system, I submitted to it and with what bored grace I could muster braced my shoulders back, pulled in my chin, and "sucked in my gut" at their commands; but I refused to go any further. I would not perform any exercises or recite any poems which much infuriated the runts with "that big plebe in F Company." They ceased to bother me when the football season began, and I got through the year finally, resolving to eliminate and discourage such performances wherever I could in the future. I think Eisenhower and Bradley and others of the Class of 1915 can attest to this when I received them for beast barracks [Plebe Summer] training in 1911.

Wood, like many cadets of character, refused to practice, and continuously opposed, the abuses and extremes of the plebe system. Even as a cadet he believed in strong discipline, but was opposed to personal hazing. Forty-nine years after he graduated from West Point in the Class of 1912, he wrote a long letter criticizing the "stupidities" of the plebe system.

There must, of course, be constant insistence on strict compliance with training requirements to meet set standards of posture and personal conduct, as emphasized in the plebe system. However, the instructions and corrections necessary to accomplish this at the service academies should not be imparted to new cadets by third classmen. Second and first classmen are more mature and responsible, and are much less likely to employ peurile sarcasm and humiliation in handling newcomers to the corps of cadets.

With a college degree already to his credit, and with a naturally bright, even brilliant, and retentive mind, the West Point academics did not challenge Wood; in fact, in his own words, he found them something of a "bore." Because he got along so easily—he graduated 12th in his class—he was frequently called upon to coach or help less gifted friends and classmates; many future generals owed their careers to him. It was this labor of love that earned him the nickname that followed him through the Army: the cadet cognomen of "P"—"P" for Professor.

In his memoirs, Wood recalled:

West Point at the turn of the century had changed little since the Civil War. New cadet barracks and a new gymnasium had been added but there was not much difference in the daily life of the Corps of Cadets. Awakened in the dark of winter mornings by the boom of the reveille gun and the shrill music of the "Hell cats"—the fifes and drums of the Army band—the cadets rubbed the sleep out of their eyes and struggled down to reveille roll call in the area of Barracks at 5:30 a.m. From then on until the last note of taps at ten, their hours were ordered and filled with classes and exercises and studies—all designed to produce a cadet worthy of the great tradition of the "Long Gray Line" that had gone before. Cadets had few privileges, even the upper-classmen; the plebes or fourth classmen had none.

Instruction in dancing was given by Monsieur Vizet with his, "One, two, cut, and glide"; and

51

Saturday night hops were held for which upper-classmen could invite young ladies. After a plebe had qualified for dancing under Monsieur Vizet, he was considered finished insofar as the social graces were concerned. Any other refinements had to be obtained by a sort of osmosis during the next three years.

The Corps of Cadets was small at that time as it had been for many years before. Until 1911, with the entry of the Class of 1915, it rarely numbered more than four hundred cadets, and the members of the various classes were pretty well acquainted with one another. Even the plebes had a rather intimate knowledge of the graduating class, particularly if prominent in athletics. Normally they were "recognized" by their team-mates prior to the completion of the plebe years. My friendship with George Patton began in my plebe year. He and I had belonged to the same college fraternity, Kappa Alpha Southern, and he came round to shake hands with me early in the year.

Deflation of egos, which may be needed in some cases, can be obtained best by rigid, aloof, impersonal insistence on conformity to the set requirements for the discipline of fourth classmen. Individual hazing has no place in the formation of true military character. In my opinion, the quality known as West Point integrity and character is developed in spite of the plebe system, rather than by it. Furthermore, the combination of the emotional strain of the plebe system and the rigid academic requirements of the first year has eliminated or turned back all too many valuable youngsters at West Point. Relieved of humiliation and undue strain, many such men have gone on to distinguished careers in the Army where sensitive, intense natures are needed as well as the thicker-skinned, hard boiled types. The formation of a young officer in our academies should produce a self-reliant, well balanced, deeply patriotic individual with a broad basic education and with great pride in his chosen profession as a leader of our armed forces. His novitiate should be akin to that of entry into a brotherhood of knights—rigid, exacting, firm, intense, on a solid basis of pride, sacrifice and devotion. The plebe and doolie systems fall far short of these ideals. Why should their stupidities be perpetuated?

This letter, a copy of which was sent to General Dwight D. Eisenhower, then in retirement at Gettysburg after two terms as President, elicited an amusing response:

My own observations and reflections on the results of the antiquated plebe system very accurately parallel your own. However, so far as my personal experience was concerned, the effects on *me* were not what some of the "runt corporals" hoped to produce. I came to West Point after having gone through, following my high school graduation, two years of hard and continuous work. I was earning a living and planning to continue to do so while I was in college, as I then hoped to be. I was practically twenty-one years old as I entered West Point. As a consequence, by the time beast barracks was over, I was beginning to see the humor in the antics of some of the ambitious as they endeavored mightily to impress their importance upon a dumb "ducrot!" There was at least a group of four of us F Company plebes who devised and sometimes carried out schemes and plots to upset and disturb those who seemed to us to be so self-impressed . . . . I was a plebe in the 20th Division when you [Wood] were a first classman in the 24th— as I remember. One day one of my cronies and I came under the disapproving eye of Corporal Elmer Adler and since he did not have time at the moment to reduce us to a proper state of humility and embarrassment, he gave us an order to come to his room that evening, in these words, "Immediately after tattoo inspection you will come to my room in Full Dress Coats." My companion, who I think must have been somewhat more imaginative than myself, came to me to discuss the exact wording of this order and proposed that we should obey it, literally.

Consequently right after 9:30 inspection, he and I came down from plebe heaven to walk into Adler's room, completely naked except for our Full Dress Coats. The roommate of Adler was Louis Byrnes, who as you may recall, was quite an indifferent and sloppy cadet. As the two startled yearlings saw us make our entry into the room, one, Adler, let out a scream that I am quite sure was heard by everyone throughout the Division. Byrnes started laughing and couldn't stop. The commotion brought into the room every upper classman of the second and third floors, and they were about equally divided in sentiment. One half thought we were so guilty of insubordination, lack of respect and dignity that we should immediately be severely disciplined—and said so!! The other half could not seem to avoid joining Byrnes. As usual, the yearling corporal had the last word! Of course he had to let us go to our rooms for taps inspection, but before we did he gave us an order in a far more detailed fashion. We were told to be back in his room immediately after taps, dressed in complete parade uniform, with guns, cross belts, tar buckets and all the rest. When we came back we executed the manual of arms for quite a spell. However, we carried along one slight evidence of victory; Byrnes was still laughing. Moreover, since this corporal was not a runt we did not get skinned!

Later, after General Wood's death, Eisenhower recalled that during his plebe year Wood, then a first classman (senior), used to stage impromptu boxing matches between plebes in his cadet room.

...he would have several of us come to his room where he would match each two of us, according to weight, for short boxing bouts, employing heavily padded practice gloves. One evening he matched my roommate and me because we were almost identical in size. We were both athletically inclined and went after each other with great vim. My opponent that evening, P. Hodgson, not only remained my roommate for four years, but after the bout was over he and I never again put on the gloves against each other.

Looking back from the vantage point of many years General Wood wrote that in the cadet years there was little evidence of future military greatness among most of those who were his associates.

The classes between 1909 and 1915 produced many general officers who carried the burden of the war [World War II] mainly in the combat grades of corps and division commanders.

But of them all only Patton made a particular impression in their cadet days upon Wood:

The quirks and vicissitudes and slings of fortune, outrageous or otherwise, cannot be predicted. Of the four members of 1909 who became army and army group commanders in the Second World War only George Patton was particularly outstanding in his military qualities as a cadet. George was Cadet Adjutant in his first class year and, except for his voice which was high-pitched and slightly quavering, he was the beau ideal of what a cadet adjutant should be — tall, erect, immaculate, and correct in all his actions. The others — Devers, Eichelberger, and Simpson — were cadet officers but of no particular academic or military distinction. I consider Eichelberger and Devers to have been a cut above the others in their wartime performance. Jake Devers, in my opinion, is probably the greatest of our leaders, except MacArthur [General of the Army Douglas MacArthur, Class of 1903] in this war [World War II] ; but he never sought publicity and little is heard or known of his achievements.

Wood's cadet years at West Point had a major influence in the making of a soldier and the shaping of a leader. Despite his well-developed self-confidence, his maverick ways, his moral courage which gave him the strength to row against the tide, Cadet Wood was a more impressionable youth than he ever admitted, and West Point forever won his heart.

The training, the inculcation, the atmosphere, the traditions, confirmed and developed Wood's strong character traits; "Duty, Honor, Country," became a life-long obligation. The service academies—West Point in particular—have long envisaged their role as both more and less than conventional educational institutions. West Point's mission is to mold and develop character, as well as to educate, to indoctrinate cadets with the love of country and of service, to produce not merely students but soldier leaders equipped to follow a professional military career. The simple commandments—"a cadet does not lie, cheat, or steal," nor does he tolerate others who do—was, and is, a solemn law to West Point. "Honor" means what the word implies. Wood wrote in his memoirs:

> There was no written cadet code of honor in my cadet days but the unwritten one, handed down for more than a century, was rigid and uncompromising and completely understood. It allowed no deviation from the exact truth in official statements, and the cadet's "All right" given to any sentinel meant that he had in no way violated any regulation in his going and coming. The code was enforced by the cadets themselves in stern fashion. An unofficial first class "vigilance committee" acted on reported cases and settled them unofficially, even requiring at times the submission of a cadet's resignation from the Academy, and its decisions were carried out.

In those four years as a cadet from 1908 to 1912, Wood merged forever with "The Long Gray Line":

They are here in ghostly assemblage,
The men of the Corps long dead,
And our hearts are standing attention

While we wait for their passing tread.

We sons of today, we salute you,
You, sons of an earlier day,
We follow, close order, behind you,
Where you have pointed the way;
The long gray line of us stretches
Thro' the years of a century told,
And the last man feels to his marrow
The grip of your far off hold.

But the big husky cadet—"a strong fellow, like an oak tree with muscles of iron"—left his own deep impression on the Point and its traditions. His great bass voice—"the greatest I've ever heard outside of opera," a fellow cadet recalled—sang "The Corps" for the first time and made it forever a part of the Military Academy's traditions. Nearly all who knew him then remember him well, as an athlete and a scholar, but, above all, as a leader. His outgoing warmth left an ineradicable impression—"When he came into a room, you knew he was there."

Before his four years were over, Wood's course was clear. This man was a natural leader.

Wood graduated high in his class, full of honors, academically, militarily, and as an athlete. He played four years of football, and was a letter man on the Varsity team. He also earned his letters on the West Point boxing and wrestling teams. He was bright and quick and intelligent, with the slow grace of a big athlete, self-confident, loyal, but more to those he commanded and those he respected than in an abstract sense; he had a keen sense of humor, a pulsing vitality, and a questioning, curious mind. The same dislike for "regimentation" with which Wood had entered West Point stayed with him through his years at the Academy, although he accommodated himself to the then spartan life of a cadet and the conformity of thought and action which the inflexible routine and ordered curriculum imposed.

Late in life Wood was to see his days at West Point through the haze of memory as one of the most satisfying periods of his life. Even if one discounts the natural tendency of age to remember youth with the glow of years, it is clear that

Wood's cadet days at West Point and his later tours of duty there shaped the man, body and soul.

My service at West Point after graduation covered three tours of duty and a span of twenty years. I went back in 1912 to assist Joe Stilwell, afterward Vinegar Joe of Burma and China fame, in coaching the ends of that year's team. In 1916 I began a tour as an instructor in Chemistry which was cut short by the war and in 1931 I went back as Deputy Commandant of Cadets.

In spite of the austerity and somewhat boring rigidity of my cadet days, it has always been a deeply pleasing and satisfying thing to return to West Point. In its subtle and unique way it left me forever under its spell and its stamp. The age-old granite hills with their historic associations and their lovely setting along the broad sweep of the Hudson together with the stately buildings, old and new, that seemed to be part of them have always been a delight to me. No other place in our country could have given a more magnificent and fitting setting for our Military Academy.

And in no other place are enshrined and preserved and enriched the history and the proud traditions of our Army and of the country itself. From the first green shoots of reluctant spring among the snow patches of the hills to the leafy beauty of summer, the bright colors of fall, and the snow-covered Plain in winter, there is an aura of strength and dignity and permanence that impresses even the casual visitor and satisfies the souls of those who spent there the golden days of youth.

★ 4 ★

THE DIVISION
Rapid Flanking Movement

THE GENERAL
Growth of a Leader

★ THE DIVISION ★

ON 12 AUGUST 1944, THE 4TH ARMORED DIVISION'S
CC A (Combat Command A) stormed into Nantes, led
through the minefields by guides from the French Resistance
Movement. Three days later the division turned over the
responsibility for containing Lorient to another unit, and
the great drive to the east started, with the division now
assigned to the XII Corps.

It was an assignment that the old Yellowlegs would
have welcomed. XII Corps was the right flank of the Third
Army, the Third Army was the right, or south flank of the
entire Allied expeditionary force in France, and the 4th
Armored Division was the right flank of the Corps. Between
the southern flank of the rampaging tankers and the Swiss-
Italian frontier there was nothing but retreating German units
and the FFI (the French Resistance Movement).

As the 4th opened its great wheeling movement to the
east, Allied units landed on the Mediterranean coast of
France in a drive that, weeks hence, was ultimately to bring
them into position on the right flank of the Third Army. But
German units defending the Mediterranean coast, their position
endangered by the Normandy breakout, had already started a
tactical withdrawal to the north when the Mediterranean

61

landings occurred on 15 August. Some of these units, pulling back hastily to Germany, were retreating across the path 4th Armored was to follow. What followed General Wood was to write about later, with some of the wry humor characteristic of the man:

Having convinced Troy Middleton and George Patton of the futility of keeping an armored division sitting in front of Lorient on the Atlantic while the Germans were moving toward their Siegfried Line on the Rhine, I was finally cut loose to move eastward north of the Loire toward objectives that could have been attained ten days before. I ordered Bruce Clarke [Commanding CC A] to clear Nantes and to move on to Orleans with his combat command and arranged for Holmes Dager [Commanding CC B] to follow with his command as soon as relieved . . . . During this period I spent much of my time in the air watching my columns which were initially about 260 miles apart and visiting the higher headquarters concerned. Holmes E. Dager made a remarkable move in closing up in thirty-six hours. Meanwhile Clarke had moved into Orleans and cleared the way for the 35th Division to take over while we again rolled east toward the Meuse, liberating town after town enroute, taking many prisoners and destroying or scattering many German formations. We were across the Meuse on 31 August ready and anxious to move on to the Moselle when the supply of gasoline ran short.

During these operations from Normandy and Brittany across France, we encountered every sort of welcome from the French people, ranging from the imperturbable and somewhat resentful attitude of Normandy to the active and valuable assistance of the numerous forces of the FFI (Forces Françaises de l'Interieure) in Brittany, the wild enthusiasm in the towns west of the Saar, and the rather ill-concealed resentment and dislike of the populations west of the Rhine. In many towns French flags broke out immediately, and our columns were showered with all sorts of gifts from flowers to sometimes over-ripe vegetables and bottles of wine. One of my officers lost his front teeth when an over-enthusiastic greeter tossed him a bottle of vintage champagne.

Moving as we did, we were often far out of reach from higher headquarters by ordinary means of communication, and . . . George Patton used his motorized "household cavalry" [termed by some "Patton's Spies"] to try to find out where we were and what we were doing. We captured thousands of prisoners, many of whom we could only disarm and send back along the roads without guard and with their hands over their heads. In Brittany, the scene of many indescribable atrocities during the occupation, some of these prisoners were disposed of by the population in accordance with their own ideas of summary justice, and officials of the International Red Cross also joined in pursuing us to find out why. Also my 10th Armored Infantry under Arthur West had captured all the funds of a German Army paymaster in millions of bright French banknotes and had scattered them throughout the countryside in every conceivable fashion, throwing packages of them to weeping French women along the roadsides, and lining their vehicles with the pretty pictures. It was not until much later that some more astute soldiers realized that they were real money and began sending them home by exchange for money orders. Thus inspectors from Supreme Headquarters [SHAEF] now joined in the chase and pestered me about who was going to pay for it all, whenever they could find me. They wanted to take it out of Art West's pay, and it was not until after the war that I finally convinced them that it had better be written off and forgotten. The Red Cross people must have made some report about the alleged massacre of prisoners, but I have never seen it and assume that we were cleared.

An open flank—a peril for infantry—was meat for the armored. General Wood had "Opie" Weyland's "recce" planes and fighter-bombers cruising constantly overhead, covering his open flank, spying out the lay of the land, warning of enemy concentrations.

Wood, like Patton, did not worry about his flanks or his communications. He echeloned his armored columns in depth, so that if a flank of a unit in the van was threatened he could quickly extend his frontage and support his leading elements. The 4th Armored virtually never used land wire for communications to the rear; they moved too fast, and some elements were often out of radio range. Relays were used. Air reconnaissance and Morse Code—the old telegrapher's "CW" or "tap-tap"—were commonplace. Usually, however, Wood "gave order to his . . . commanders orally and in person . . . . Every commander was able to recognize another's voice over the field radio." This increased security and simplified control.

The 4th Armored established a liaison with its supporting XIX Tactical Air Command under General O. P. ("Opie") Weyland that was probably unique. Wood trusted completely in Weyland's air cover and Weyland in turn trusted him. The air rode "shotgun" over, beside, and ahead of the tanks; there were few ambushes or surprises as a result. General Weyland recently wrote:

> XIX TAC had air liaison parties with 4th Armored and its combat commands. These air officers normally rode in lead tanks with direct radio communications to recce and fighter bomber flights operating in advance and on the flanks of advancing ground force units. (We called this "armored column cover").
>
> 4th Armored became one of our favorite outfits. They took immediate and full advantage of friendly air power and didn't whimper if they got a bloody nose in an engagement. Air-Ground teamwork was terrific. Example: Late one afternoon a 4th Armored CC was preparing to bivouac for the night. A fighter bomber flight was operating against German troops 15-20 miles ahead when one of our pilots was shot

down, but got out of his plane unhurt, though close to the Germans. The flight commander reported the predicament to the air liaison officer on the ground with the CC. 4th Armored unhesitatingly fought on ahead and picked up the downed pilot. This was air-ground teamwork *we* appreciated.

Example: Patton was death on looting of private property—however, Wermacht military supplies were legitimate and covered quite a range of items. 4th Armored was noted for its scrounging, and usually found time to screen the contents of German military warehouses and depots they overran. XIX TAC units periodically received consignments of such supplies for test and evaluation—examples being German pistols, cases of cognacs and champagnes (methodically labelled "Reserved for the Wermacht—forbidden for sale"), and less frequently, fresh commissary meats.

The "big, tough" Thunderbolt F-47's roared over the armored spearheads almost continuously, linked by radio to the air support officer on the ground:

Yellow Leader, Yellow Leader; this is Eggcup— Do you see our column, 1,000 yards north of the crossroads?

The vehicles of "Eggcup" (the XIX TAC designation for the 4th Armored Division and the air controllers assigned to work with it) would display identification panels to distinguish friend from foe, and "Yellow Leader" (planes of the XIX TAC) would be coached to the attack by the air liaison officer in a lead tank.

Few calls for air support went without response. A great mutual respect between air and ground, bred in the confidence Wood inspired and the understanding of "Opie" Weyland, rapidly burgeoned.

... [Wood] used to send back to the pilots of a fighter group who had given him particular help, a truck load of [captured] brandy.

The trading of bulky fur lined flying jackets for the

65

blanket lined tanker jackets caused a problem through the Third Army-XIX TAC area but it showed the love of one fighting man for his brother each of whom thought the other had the tougher job.

The teamwork between XIX TAC and 4th Armored Division was probably as close or closer in spirit, and superior in quality, to that in any other Army operation in World War II, and was not, indeed, to be equalled again until the Vietnamese war, twenty years later. A great deal of this successful liaison was due to General Wood's understanding of the uses of air power, and also to his respect for General Weyland and his staff.

Roger J. Browne, now a Major General, USAF retired, who was then A-3 to Weyland, also deserves a major share of the credit for this successful partnership. Wood, while in training in England, initially had the concept of most ground officers: that air squadrons should be parcelled out to ground commanders. Browne quotes him as saying at Salisbury Plain, "Son, I want you to give me one of your fighter groups and with my Armored Division I'll blast my way through those Krauts." Wood and "Eggcup" quickly came to realize, however, that dispersion of air resources was not the best way to get results. In retrospect after the war, as Browne put it,

> There were too many aviators who were saying that air power made the invasion of Europe possible and the invasion of Japan unnecessary.
>
> Equally, there were too many doughboys and tankers who were saying that man is the ultimate weapon and that wars are won on the ground. Both philosophies are partially right; I was trying to moderate both stands.

The great flanking movement of the 4th Armored started like a scythe, flailing a wide arc across the dusty roads of France, first towards Orleans and the Loire, then on to the east and north. The tanks and jeeps high-tailed, barrelling along with scattered bursts of gunfire and occasional brief halts. The two combat commands started to drive into the heart of France some 200 miles apart; CC B moved 264 miles in 34 hours; CC A roared from Nantes to St. Calais in 22 hours, fueled up, and drove towards Orleans. Orleans, the historic city of Joan of Arc and *point d'appui* and anchor of the Paris-Orleans gap—a traditional invasion route into the heart of France—fell "in sharp fighting over mined streets" to the 4th Armored on 16 August, one day after the great drive started.

There was no halt. The scythe swung on. CC A took Sens on the Yonne River, 70 miles east of Orleans and southeast of Paris, on 21 August, and captured Troyes on the Seine River, far to the east of Paris on 26 August.

The assault elements, as they had been taught, by-passed the strongly held positions and wasted no time in rebuilding blown bridges, finding other river crossings instead. When towns or strongpoints could not be by-passed they were taken in stride, with sudden, headlong assault and bruising power.

Tactics, reminiscent of the cavalry charges of the past, dominated the battle for Troyes. A company of medium tanks, armored infantrymen in half-tracks, and self-propelled assault howitzers—about 800 men—staged a "Charge of the Light Brigade." Over three and a half miles of open ground, the armor rumbled down a gentle slope into Troyes where 2,000 to 3,000 Germans, including the 51st SS Brigade, were dug in. In "desert" formation, spread out with 100 yards between vehicles, "engines roaring at full throttle," the tankers went all out. German artillery fire burst near them. As the open half-tracks "galloped" towards the German defenses they "hunted" the enemy shell bursts, veering like ships in a seaway to throw off the German gunners' aim.

The sheer audacity and momentum of the charge carried the day. The tanks leaped a seven foot anti-tank ditch, breaking down the soft earth and cleaning out the enemy enfilading positions. The tanks, protected by the armored infantrymen who mopped up anti-tank crews and bazooka gunners, rambled through the streets, shooting up pockets of resistance with high explosives and white phosphorus. It was a sharp, nasty little fight, which ended in Wagnerian thunder at dawn on 26 August when 4th Armored Division tanks shot up a German ammunition column attempting to escape the city, and armored infantry ambushed a relief column. Some

533 Germans were killed and 557 captured. Troyes, a position that might have been a tough nut to crack, fell quickly to the sheer impetuosity and drive of the tankers.

The scythe swung on. The ancient river barriers of France, which had run red with blood in another war, were rapidly reached and crossed. Before the end of the month, the armored spearheads of the 4th had crossed the Marne; as September opened, they were across the Meuse, lumbering past "moldering, weed-grown trenches and shell craters through towns whose names rang with the history of World War I.

In this "hell-for-leather" drive across France, the man with the most headaches in the 4th Armored Division was G-4, the Assistant Chief of Staff for Supply. Wood never let supplies dominate operations; he expected his G-4 to conform to his plans. The "Book" was abandoned; the situation called for innovation and got it. Hal C. Pattison, then a Lieutenant Colonel, wrote later:

> Very early in the game it was learned that the only sure way to have supplies when you needed them on an operation of penetration or exploitation was to take them with you. Accordingly, the command had made a practice of carrying along every available truck loaded with supplies. Every kitchen truck was stripped of its mess equipment and loaded with gas or ammunition. Rations were carried on the combat vehicles. Every supply truck was loaded to more than 100% overload, and indeed some trucks carried as much as seven to eight tons of supplies. Whenever possible . . . an extra truck platoon from an attached truck company was attached to the trains. The trains [supply vehicles] were never left behind to be brought up later; they followed immediately behind the combat column, and that proved to be the safest place for them. They could follow along in the vacuum created by the shock of the combat column and be safely through the enemy resistance before it could recover.

The tankers took their lumps; victories such as their's cannot be won without paying the price of blood. German rocket-firing planes hit the 4th's bridgehead across the Meuse,

68

south of St. Mihiel on 1 September, killing six men and wounding 57. But the Germans paid. Nine planes were shot down, and the armored artillery caught retreating German columns over their sights and clobbered the enemy.

The engineers came into their own, as the successive rivers were crossed. Blown bridges were replaced, fords established; the supplies must keep rolling. In a paper prepared for the Army's Command and General Staff College Lieutenant Colonel Pattison later reported:

> The 4th Armored had been burning captured fuel and gasoline flown in by transport planes. Maps and shells, as well, had been flown to the racing tank columns. When the overall gasoline supply problem became critical, higher headquarters halted the big drive [just ten miles from the Moselle River].
>
> This was the end of the line—out of maps and out of gas, the command [CC A] was to remain in this position until 12 September. The road was clear ahead, the Moselle River was still undefended and the road to Germany was open but even the most willing hands cannot drag a Sherman tank. This enforced delay was to cause us much suffering and many casualties in the coming months.
>
> The division had run a marathon at sprint speed. In the seven weeks since Normandy, the 4th Armored had thrown a 700-mile right hook across the heart of France. Tanks put more than 1,500 miles on their speedometers in leading Third Army's drive to the Moselle. Truck drivers at the wheels of their overloaded 6 by 6's day and night rolled more than 3,000 miles to supply the division . . . .

And, on 11 September, just a few days later, as fall came to an embattled Europe and the Allies threatened the citadel of Germany, reconnaissance elements of the Third Army and of the U.S. Seventh Army, advancing from the Mediterranean beaches, met far to the south near Dijon.

The door had swung shut.

★ THE GENERAL ★

WOOD GRADUATED FROM WEST POINT INTO A TIGHT-knit little Army, an army of somewhat narrow professionals, whose military values and tradition were just commencing to be shaken by the advent of the truck, the field radio and the plane.

To Wood, who until the days of armor never developed the intense branch consciousness that limited the usefulness of so many officers of the old army, new ideas were the wine of life. As a young officer he had the great advantage of frequent transfer from post to post and branch to branch. He avoided, therefore, the stultification, the ossification, the excessive branch loyalty, that the ingrown nature of much Army life then fostered.

Wood was commissioned in the Coast Artillery Corps. Later he shifted to Ordnance, then to Field Artillery, and, finally, as an artillery officer he found his crowning role in Armor. The young officer, who read widely in military history, was greatly influenced by the traditions of the old cavalry and even more by the old field artillery. He was commissioned into an Army of horses; he rode and played polo, and he thought in terms of fire and movement— particularly movement.

70

But he retained his singularity; he paid obeisance to no man's thought, but tried to build his own military philosophy. Years later, he was to write:

I studied military lore deeply and extensively after leaving West Point, reading of campaigns and captains in hundreds of tomes and in the five languages which I am able to understand.* But of all that, no single word or thought moved me unless it conformed to my own instinct and understanding, and no military leader except Robert E. Lee ever seemed to me worthy of my whole-hearted admiration and emulation.

It was a small Army in that end of the golden age prior to World War I, and Wood met again and again at the Army posts and at West Point (where he returned to teach and to coach football) the men he had known as cadets, men who were to come to the brief fame of military glory a war later: "Joe" Stilwell, "Crit" Crittenberger, "Jeff" Keyes, and many others. Wood had the faculty—rare in men—of making great friendships. Those of his time at West Point who survive love him to this day. But with this gift he coupled an even rarer quality: the ability, despite his love for a friend, to see the man clearly, objectively. It is a kind of second sight, embarrassing and not always an asset, to him who possesses it.

In World War I, Wood first came in contact with the citizen soldier, the amateur, the modern Minuteman, who in all of America's wars has come to the defense of his country. At Augusta, Georgia, he "tried to teach a group of selected young men from the University of Pennsylvania and Wharton Business School, among them Thom McCabe [later chairman of the Board of the Federal Reserve Bank] and Leon Henderson [later a famous economist and prominent adviser in the 'New Deal' administration of Franklin D. Roosevelt], the fundamentals of military discipline and service." He learned there

_____

*Wood, a natural linguist, acquired, in the course of his career, a reading capability, and some spoken capability, in French, German, Spanish and Russian, as well as English.

Fall of 1912. 2nd Lt. Wood (front row, seated, 1st on left) as football coach (ends & tackles) at West Point with rest of coaching staff.

how to get along with the citizen in uniform; he formed an admiration for most of them--"none of them ever let me down."

As a Major (promotion was briefly fast in the few bloody months in which the United States participated in that great "crusade for democracy") Wood went to France as ordnance officer of the 3rd Division. But not before he lived through scenes which left on his memory a kind of Hogarthian patina of horror.

The winter of 1917 was unusually cold and rainy in the South. At times, the seas of mud in the camps were so deep that wagons and trucks could not move, and supplies had to be packed by mule train. Influenza became epidemic, followed by measles. Young lads just inducted died by the hundreds, and the dismal roll of drums as their bodies were carried to railhead for shipment home seemed interminable from dawn to dusk . . . .

Decimated before embarkation, the 3rd Division nevertheless absorbed its replacements and reached France in time for Chateau Thierry and the final five months of bitter

combat of World War I. Like so many of that young genera-
tion of the American Expeditionary Force, the seed bed of
the leaders of World War II, Wood was sent to the staff
college at Langres, France, where French and British officers,
veterans of three years of war, tried to impart their knowledge of the enemy and of modern conflict to the young and
eager men from across the sea. Wood was in the same class
at Langres as George Patton (throughout their careers, the
paths of these two men crossed and re-crossed), and with
Simpson, and "Sandy" Patch (Lieutenant General Alexander

World War I, 1917. Major
Wood as Ordnance Officer of
the 3rd U.S. Infantry Division
(Wood transferred from the
Coast Artillery Corps to the
Ordnance Corps in order to
get overseas.)

Patch, in World War II commander of the U.S. Seventh Army), all to rise to high rank a quarter of a century later. With him, too, were the "citizen soldiers": Henry W. Stimpson and Dwight Davis, both of whom were to become Secretaries of War.

We studied hard at Langres, but the place was not without its pleasures. Most of us were young and had just come out of combat with the prospect of early return, so we made the most of them. I remember one evening when George Patton and a few of us kindred souls visited the British mission and found the members crying over their drinks. It seemed that an old hunting tradition had been profaned by the French people in Langres who had captured a wild boar and had it penned up in a butcher-shop pending ignominious slaughter. We joined in their drinks and their unrestrained grief over such an end for a noble *sanglier,* and the decision was made to liberate him from the *boucherie* and hunt him down to a proper death through the streets of Langres. The action was immediate—the door of the shop was forced and the beast was loosed, followed by our band of huntsmen giving tongue with correct cries of Yoicks and the View-Hallow—all pursued by a puzzled gendarme discharging his pistol into the air at odd moments. The kill was finally made in a corner of the cathedral with knives taken from the butcher-shop; the gendarme was appeased; the shop-owner reimbursed; honor was saved—and all was well. The verdict of the citizens of Langres was unanimous: "Comme ils sont fous, les Allies!"

Wood went back to the front lines and served as staff officer of the 90th Division at St. Mihiel. The quick German collapse of November 1918, was unexpected, and shortly before the Armistice some young veterans of the fighting were detached and sent back to the United States to help staff the new divisions then forming, which were expected to participate in the battles of 1919. Wood, on Armistice Day, was Assistant Chief of Staff, G-4, of the 18th Division at San Antonio, and, as such, for the first but not the last time in his life, he saw the United States tear down and break apart the giant structure of security it had so carefully built.

The Great War was over. An era was ended—an era beginning in relative peace and contentment in our country and ending in blood, death, destruction and world unrest. Nothing would ever again be the same, or even similar.

But this was retrospect; he was not to know then the sense of frustration which later beset so many Americans who found the "Great Crusade" led only to a lost peace.

Professionally, Wood's service in World War I contributed materially to his education in the mobile concepts in which he was later to excel. He saw, in France, the trench stalemate and the triumph of the machine gun, which had hobbled movement and had forced a static, linear conflict. He saw, too, the advent of the tank and the development of the plane, and his eager mind read and absorbed the thoughts of many military writers, impatient with static warfare and static ideas. He commenced to seek and search for a better way to win wars than "by chewing on barbed wire in Flanders," to paraphrase Winston Churchill's words. Later Wood noted:

Back to normalcy was the post-war slogan, and back to normalcy the post-war Army went, struggling to keep alive a flickering flame and faltering spirit of national preparedness, struggling to maintain and modernize its arms and equipment, and struggling for its very life to obtain the funds necessary for its meager existence. Back it went to promotions few and far between, to small posts and small units, and to the apathy that follows periods of high endeavor.

My next twenty years or more of Army life were those of the usual peacetime assignments for a field officer of Field Artillery (in the comradeship of many close and wonderful, and sometimes, inspiring friends) . . .

Those were . . . years in which there was time for study and quiet reflection on the nature of war and the shape of wars to come. George Patton, with whom I served at Leavenworth [formerly a cavalry post and site of the Army's Command and General Staff School] and Hawaii, possessed a splendid library of military works, and we read everything from the maxims of Sun Tsu and Confucius to the latest articles in our own and foreign military publications. We often sat, glass in hand, arguing loud and long on war, ancient and modern, with its battles and commanders. George's delightful wife, Bea, used to stand it as long as she could and then retire, saying she had never heard two people argue more vociferously on the same side of all questions.

This was a period, in the U.S. Army, of dichotomy and conflict, of clinging to the past and looking to the future. Throughout the 1920's and 1930's horsed cavalry, horsed field artillery, and even mule packtrains still vied with the tank and the motor truck. It was hard, even for the exceptional officer, to put the dead past behind him, for to the polo-playing, horse-loving Army of the period between wars there was an elan, a tradition, about the horse. Wood felt it; he was, indeed, a product of the military era of the horse. He commanded a horse-drawn artillery outfit in North Carolina in the 1920's and wrote about it afterwards:

> There was nothing more delightful than to move out at the head of my battalion of 75's in the cool of a frosty morning, guns and caissons rolling, horses snorting, and trace-chains rattling as we trotted along the sandy roads, preceded by a cloud of battery dogs ranging like scouts far and wide ahead. When T-Bone, and Hamfat, the short-legged terriers of B Battery tired of this, they would wait for their battery at the side of the road where they were picked up and installed on the saddles of the wheel-drivers. One of my first orders on joining the outfit was that not *all* dogs were required to attend *all* formations and that they would *not* be present at ceremonies, including retreat—an order which caused the first sergeants much anguish, I am sure.

But Wood knew the day of the horse was ended; he appended to this passage of "things remembered," a note in long-hand:

76

Culver, Indiana 1936. R.O.T.C. duty at Culver Military Academy. Major Wood on his thoroughbred mare "Clear Faith" - sister of "Man-Of-War".

C'est magnifique, mais ce n'etait pas la guerre — the horse artillery!

In this period between wars Wood always sought troop command. He avoided staff duty and Washington like the plague and even begged off an assignment to the Army War College in favor of duty in the field. He did attend the staff college at Leavenworth, and the French Ecole Superieur de Guerre, and had a brief artillery refresher course at Fort Sill.

Wood also had an unusually long span of ROTC duty — almost 10 years: 5 years at Culver Military Academy and 5 years at the University of Wisconsin. This helped him materially, not only in developing his concepts of leadership but in aiding him to understand the psychology of the citizen soldier, the civilian in uniform, who was to form in World War II the greatest Army that had been mustered in the history of the world.

Wood continued to develop through practice and experience the natural traits of a leader he had exhibited since his youth, and to evolve through study and reflection the professional ideas and command methods he later employed in battle. He was a man who was never willing to relapse into static thought; a close friend, Lieutenant General Willis D. Crittenberger, recalled later that Wood was,

> . . . always writing . . . letters about the use of artillery.
>
> He was a fast moving fellow; he was restless and he wanted to go.

But Wood was not one who suffered fools gladly and he did not fit easily into the rigid framework of the traditional concept of a soldier—"Their's not to question why . . . ." Wood was always questioing why, and he was sometimes frankly bored with duties that he considered did not contribute to the development of military effectiveness.

He recalled, years afterwards, that he had once been called in by the late Colonel H. L. Newbold, when Wood was executive to Colonel Newbold in the 8th Field Artillery. The Colonel told Wood he had rated him

> . . . superior [in a fitness report] on all counts except as "Post Dump Officer."
>
> He said he was required to show me this for comment, as he had been forced to rate me "below average" in this regard. I thanked him and said that I had one comment and one request to make in the matter:
>
> "I would much appreciate your changing that rating to 'Inferior.' There is nothing I would like better in the Army than being known as an *Inferior Post-Dump Officer.*"

Wood's dry humor and his propensity for displaying a sophistication superior to his fellows, though rarely offensive, sometimes earned him a friendly rebuke in kind. After his course at the Ecole de Guerre Wood attended a two weeks refresher course at the Field Artillery School at Fort Sill, Oklahoma. Most of the curriculum was "old-hat" to him.

> . . . he pretended to be above instruction when in class-

room sessions he would unfold a newspaper and be absorbed in reading it . . . he was asked to present a brief. As he stepped to the lectern each classmate opened a newspaper and buried himself in it. "P" took it with a grin and carried out his mission.

Thus Wood continued to develop and to harden, in the period between the wars, the personality and character traits which had impressed his fellow cadets at West Point. He was in many ways a military iconoclast, with ideas of his own and the moral courage to express them. But they were not ideas forged in a vacuum; they burgeoned from long study. He was a natural leader, born and bred, outstanding in any company, physically strong, with enormous vitality and energy, and a physical and mental restlessness which could be slacked only by vigorous bodily activity, sports of all types and by study or discussion.

He had weaknesses, like all men born, among them little toleration or respect for men of lesser minds or small characters. Sometimes, if he felt he or his were unjustly put upon, he expressed his dissent in terms so vigorous as to seem, given the strict hierarchy of military rank, almost insubordinate. But he was not insubordinate; he carried out orders and paid formal obeisance to the symbols of authority; he departed from accepted protocol only when he was convinced injustice or just plain foolishness was in control. He did not do this often, but when he did he thundered and the heavens listened.

★ 5 ★

THE DIVISION
Violent Fire and Maneuver

THE GENERAL
Division Commander

★ THE DIVISION ★

IN MID-SEPTEMBER 1944, 70 MILES FROM THE GERMAN border, the tanks of the 4th Armored smashed across a great river line of France—the Moselle River and its companion waterways. The bridges had been blown by the retreating Germans but the tankers didn't wait for the engineers; fire and momentum meant victory.

One canal had been drained but was deep in mud and muck; its steep ditch and high banks created a formidable tank barrier. A medium tank battalion used its 75mm guns to break down the high canal banks; hastily cut logs thrown into the mud and water provided a "bottom" for the tank tracks. The tanks found fords across the Moselle's channels, with water splashing around their turrets.

It wasn't an easy crossing. Five river channels of the Moselle and its tributaries, and two canals had to be forded, and the Germans were fighting back. The 4th took casualties; one of the wounded tankers, white-faced with shock, with a bloody compress over the stump of his left arm, tried to joke: "Well, I won't have to sweat out that CBI [China-Burma-India] deal with the rest of you guys."

By mid-September the 4th Armored had crossed the Moselle, encircled Nancy, and forced its evacuation. Combat

83

Command A's "ride around Nancy [was] comparable on a modern scale to [Jeb] Stuart's ride around Richmond [in the Civil War]," according to the Corps Commander, Major General Manton S. Eddy. The bridgehead established was the "base from which the drive against the Saar was launched in November 1944."

But the breaching of the Moselle line led to furious German reaction, and to one of the might-have-beens of history. On 15 September, the Germans had no reserves, and General Wood, champing at the bit, wanted to keep pushing along the Marne-Rhine Canal to Sarrebourg. Patton agreed and on 16 September, he ordered the XII Corps to drive rapidly northeast into the Darmstadt area and establish a bridgehead across the Rhine. But as Major General F. W. Von Mellenthin later noted in his book, *Panzer Battles*:

... the Americans failed to exploit a fine opportunity for a rapid advance to the Saar .... General Eddy, the

France, September 1944, Moselle River area. 4th Armored tanks crossing drained canal.

commander of the XII Corps, turned down a request from the 4th U.S. Armored Division, whose commander, Major General J. S. Wood, realized that . . . [the German] First Army had no reserves and could not resist a bold thrust along the Marne-Rhine Canal to Sarrebourg.

Wood was ordered to divert some of his tanks to the rear to help the 35th Division "tidy up the battlefield," and the rest of his division was "out on a limb," 15 miles in advance of any other unit immobilized by orders near Arracourt. The opportunity was lost.

On 18 September the German Fifth Panzer Army, commanded by General Hasso von Manteuffel, was personally directed by Hitler to hit the 4th Armored in flank, "retake Luneville and wipe out the American bridgeheads across the Moselle." The attack led to two weeks of vicious armored fighting—what General Wood was later to call "the greatest tank battle of the war on the Allied front."

"Furious armored counterattacks" by the Germans started on 19 September. The powerful, sleek, new "wide-tracked" Panthers, "as big as a house," with a high velocity gun that seemed "to run out there for miles," took on the 4th Armored Division's Shermans. There should have been no contest; the Sherman, especially the low velocity 75 mm model then used by the 4th Armored Division, was just no match for the German monster. But the tankers had learned their lessons well; they maneuvered to take the Panthers in the side where the German tanks were vulnerable, or they fired at the tracks to immobilize them. The tank destroyer battalion got hull down and waited to let the Panthers have it, almost until they saw "the whites of their eyes"; the armored infantry dug in, and the artillery fired over open sights at the rumbling German monsters. It was a bruising melee, but in the first four days the 113th Panzer Brigade lost about 75% of its 56 Mark V Panthers.

The vicious jabs continued, but in Wood's words, "the division rolled with the punch," and, with heavy air support from the XIX Tactical Air Command, they taught one of Germany's most successful generals a lesson in amored tactics. In the first four days, as Chester Wilmot wrote in *Struggle for Europe,* "Wood handled his armor brilliantly and dealt so severely with two of the new Panzer brigades that by 22 September both were crippled [150 tanks destroyed]."

It was on that date that the famous and controversial halt order from Eisenhower to Patton blasted Third Army's hopes that the line of the Rhine might be quickly breached. The rampaging Third, short on gasoline and supplies, was to regroup, beef up its supply lines, clean up pockets of German resistance and get its wind for another push.

It was a sad time for the tankers, who believed that speed, dash, momentum, and fire power, coupled with boldness, could win the war quickly. They felt hobbled by logistics, shortages, and cautious strategy. General "Hap" Gay recalled:

> Patton and Wood were often together, particularly so when the shortage of gasoline grew critical. One evening, just at dusk, I saw them standing alone, faced to the East, with tears in their eyes as they foresaw the awful waste of life—lives of our boys being sacrificed, unnecessarily so, by the lack of fuel for their armor . . . .

"Third U.S. Army received categorical orders to stand on the defensive . . . it certainly simplified our problems," Von Mellenthin, the German Chief of Staff of Army Group (G) later wrote, and "gave us a few week's grace to rebuild our battered forces and get ready to meet the next onslaught."

But for the 4th Armored, the halt in place meant no immediate end of fighting. Manteuffel kept trying all through the end of September; he regrouped on the 26th and, aided by the low clouds and bad weather which hampered U.S. air support, he kept driving against the 4th's positions around Arracourt. Time and again, the German Panzers rumbled towards the American positions out of the mist and rain. Time and again tanks on both sides were "brewed up" in leaping flame and smoke—often crematoriums for their crews.

It was no good. The 4th's "violent fire" broke up the Nazi attacks. When one overran a position, the U.S. units

France, September - October 1944. Wood and Patton at the front in the mud and rain.

France, 1944, Gen. Wood conferring in front of his tent with Col. Bigby, Chief of Staff, 4th Armored Division.

"rolled with the punch," and came back in counter-attack to overwhelm the enemy. On 29 September the weather cleared; the fighter-bombers of "Opie" Weyland's XIXth Tactical Air Division roared down in force and "Mantueffel's attack broke down."

"P" Wood commanded in person. He watched much of the action from his Cub plane, and he saw "burning tanks blazing all the way from the Deueze road to the Foret de Parroy."

It was a bitter slugging match but the 4th would not be licked. By the end of September the division had faced, in the Moselle-Nancy-Aracourt battles, all or part of the 11th Panzer Division, the 15th Panzer Grenadier Division, the 553rd and 558th Infantry Divisions, and the 111th and 113th Panzer Brigades. The results were discrepant: the Germans lost 281 tanks, including many of their vaunted Panthers and 67 artillery pieces; the 4th Armored Division lost about 100 vehicles of all types. The division captured more than 3,000 prisoners and killed an estimated 3,040 Germans.

> Since the beginning of your historic drive through Orleans to the east, the 4th Armored Division has met its assigned tasks with the greatest distinction . . . . In the establishing, defending and enlarging of our bridgehead across the Moselle, all members of the division have conducted themselves in a manner of which they may well be proud . . . .

All along the line from the Swiss frontier to the sea the Allied armies were halted. The "Red Ball express"—a continuous stream of trucks—was thundering across France night and day; transport aircraft were bringing up gasoline; replacements moved forward from the depots. Both sides, spent and gasping, girded for the climactic battles to come. On 12 October, after 87 days of combat, the 4th Armored Division—halted by orders, not the enemy—came out of the muddy, bloody front, for a rest.

And on 17 October, during a slack period, the Combat History of the 4th Armored Division records:

The Forward Echelon of the Division Headquarters moved from its tent offices in a field which had become almost a swamp due to the recent continuous rain into a chateau on the edge of Remerville. They were the last to seek shelter from the elements, the Division Commander being of the opinion that so long as his troops were in the field he and his staff would remain there also.

This was a miserable period of mud and rain with all the discomforts of a Northern European Winter. Through it all General Wood lived in a tent under Spartan conditions, sleeping on a cot, and showering with a stream of water from a jerry can.

Brigadier General Hal C. Pattison recollected an incident when Lieutenant General Carl ("Toohey") Spaatz, then commanding the Eighth Air Force, a life-long friend of General Wood, visited the division headquarters one day in early October, and,

> . . . on seeing the conditions under which General Wood was living, [he] sent to him [Wood], upon his return to his own headquarters, a magnificent house trailer van of the type in which the senior Air Force generals lived in the field. General Wood was inordinately proud of his van. He had it parked adjacent to the headquarters and proudly escorted visitors of all ranks through his van, showing off all of its appointments with great pleasure.
>
> At the end of a week, General Wood returned the van to General Spaatz. When people asked General Wood why he did not keep the van and live in it, his answer was "My people are living in the mud, and if they can live and fight in it, I can do work in it as well. When they get out of the mud, then I will get out of it also."
>
> "His people" always knew that he was willing to put up with the worst conditions that any of his men had faced.

The 4th Armored did not rest for long. General Abrams, then a Lieutenant Colonel, recalled this brief hiatus well:

Maj. Gen. Wood in house trailer van sent to him by
Lt. Gen. "Toohey" Spaatz. The van was never used.

In November of 1944, we were preparing for an offensive operation in Third Army, and it was to kick off
on General Patton's birthday, November the 11th. On
the 8th or 9th the commanders were all assembled at
division headquarters, and we came into a simple old
farm house there and sat down on the floor . . . and
shortly in came General Patton and General Wood.
Everyone stood up and General Patton had us sit down,
and General Wood introduced him simply, and the two
of them sat in a couple of farmhouse chairs up in the
front. General Patton talked to us; the jist of the talk
went something like this. He said, "I have come down
here tonight to be with you all, not because I want
to tell you what to do or how to do it, because," he said,
"you all know far more about it than I do." He said,
"You have exceeded anything that I could have ever ex-

pected, and so I leave the job that has to be done to you, the masters of it. What I really came down for," he said, "you know this offensive jumps off on my birthday, and I thought just being with you for a few minutes would give me confidence and renew my spirit." With that the "Old Man" got up and left. Well, it had a tremendous inspirational effect, I know, on all of us, not only for the words of the Army Commander, but for our Division Commander, who, it appeared to us, was equally respected by the Army Commander.

In early November the XII Corps jumped off again, towards Saarbrucken and the Siegfried Line—an attack, Wood thought, that "should have come in September" before the momentum was halted. It was too late.

> The cold winter rain had been falling for three weeks; Lorraine pastures were bogs, streams were rivers. Rivers ran over their banks. The Seine Valley was a wide expanse of swirling water....

The tankers fitted the duckbill grousers to their tracks and moved out through the mire. The 4th had been held out, at first, for exploitation, but the XII Corps infantry divisions were bogged down and the Corps commander committed his tanks "to retrieve the setback."

But it was a "one-tank" front; the tanks were confined to the roads, and some of them were badly shot up by 88's. Water, mud, terrain, and weather hobbled mobility. There was no room now for the wide sweeping envelopments of past months; it was again "violent fire" and movement.

The 4th took its lumps and ground ahead, slowly but steadily. General von Mellenthin, the German, was later to write:

> ...the armored divisions were committed too early and ... Eddy [Lieutenant General Manton S. Eddy, who commanded the XII Corps] would have done better to wait until his infantry had eaten away more of our main defense zone. However, the 4th Armored was a tough and experienced formation and its Combat Command B, in spite of the abominable weather,

smashed through the left flank of our 48th Division and reached Hannocourt and Viviers. Combat Command A of the same division came into action to the east of Chateau-Salins and reached Rodalbe on 11 November.

Wood later wrote that he agreed "completely" with von Mellethin's estimate, that "there was no opportunity for the maneuver of armor at which we were adept and it is surprising that we made...significant advances...."

The 4th had shown that it could take it as well as dish it out; there was bitter house-to-house fighting in Fonteny to clean up cellars and dug-in positions, and in the 48 hour battle for Guebling starting on 14 November, CC A took the heaviest artillery fire it had experienced in the war. On 16 November, the division took Morhange, leaving Via Dolorosa of blood and agony in its wake.

Then came a brief surcease from combat. Sometime in this period Wood was awarded a Bronze Star Medal. His recollections of the event typify the man:

France, near Arracourt, October 1944. Gen. Wood confers with his Corps Commander and a fellow Division Commander. l to r: Brig. Gen. Holmes Dager, CC "B", Maj. Gen. Willard S. Paul, CG 26 Inf. Div., Maj. Gen. Wood, Maj. Gen. Manton S. Eddy, CG XII Corps.

France, November 1944. Maj. Gen. Eddy confers with Maj. Gen. Wood.

While at lunch with George at his headquarters mess near Laval along with Prince Felix of Luxembourg and others he sent someone out to get a Bronze Star Medal for me. I fear I startled some of the entourage by saying that I did not want the damned thing; but George said he wanted to make the decoration "popular and sought after," as he put it, so I stuck it in my pocket and went on my way. The habit of wearing a chestful of various ribbons never appealed to me—it has become ridiculous around places such as NATO and the Pentagon and I cut the lot down to the DSC and the DSM which seemed sufficient and less burdensome and a tribute to the men who were with me. If I had been so fortunate as to earn the Medal of Honor, I would have worn no other decoration, ever.

On 19 November the Division went back into the fray again, against "mines, impassible roads, heavy artillery fire." The Combat History of the Division, under the date of 19

November, records "numerous mines in the vicinity of Rodalbe. The engineers removed an estimated 911 mines in this area . . . ."

The 4th Armored pushed clear of Fenetrange on Thanksgiving Day, but with no turkey for the tankers. The tank guns and SP's and TD's (self-propelled artillery and tank destroyers) blasted a freeway towards the Saar and by the 25th most of the division had crossed the river.

The 4th's crossing at Fenetrange took the division outside of the often sacrosanct corps and army boundaries, but, as Wood later wrote,

> . . . such lines meant little to me and I went where the going was good.
>
> It was lucky for the XV Corps that we did, for we struck in flank, the Panzer Lehr Division which had been reconstituted after we manhandled it in Normandy and ordered to move south to hit the north flank of the XV Corps under my friend and classmate, Major General [Wade H.] Haislip. As related by von Mellenthin: "On the morning of 24 November, Panzer Lehr under General Bayerlein ran into the flank cover of the XVth Corp to the north of Sarrebourg—made up of reconnaissance troops and part of the 44th U.S. Division. Bayerlein might well have broken through to the Sarrebourg-Saverna road, but unfortunately was taken in flank by the 4th Armored Division which had forced its way across the Saar at Fenetrange. Heavy fighting developed on the 24-25 November. On the afternoon of 25 November I went to Bayerlein's battle headquarters and saw for myself how precarious his situation was. Bayerlein recommended that the attack should be discontinued, and I strongly supported the request. But O. K. W. insisted that Panzerlehr persist in its hopeless task . . . . On 27 November Panzerlehr was driven back to its original jump-off line east of Sarre-Union."

At the end of the cold, dismal month of November with the landscape drowned in mud and the sky draped with clouds and mist, the 4th was east of Sarre-Union and pushing forward with "violent fire" against "fanatical resistance of the enemy, bad weather, soft terrain, heavy artillery fire."

The going had been tough. But the tankers had clobbered the enemy, dishing out far more damage than they took. During the month the division had destroyed or captured 61 enemy tanks, 104 large caliber artillery pieces, and 11 antiaircraft guns (including many of the dreaded, high velocity 88 mm), and had captured 1,095 prisoners, and killed 1,575 Germans. It had lost 36 medium and 10 light tanks, artillery pieces and 140 miscellaneous vehicles, and had 220 men K.I.A. (killed in action), 38 missing and 805 wounded. Its losses were only partly replaced; it received 836 enlisted men and 95 officers as replacements during the month. It was a month of bashing—the heaviest, most violent fire of the campaign. The division expended 67,348 rounds of large caliber ammunition and 1,405,895 rounds of small arms ammo.

It was about this time, too, that the Division and the Allied High Command became aware of the awesome reputation the 4th had in German ranks. A captured German SS colonel wanted to see General Wood to learn how the division had achieved such rapidity of advance. A SHAEF intelligence report, summarizing information gained from American prisoners freed from a German PW camp at Strasbourg, noted that,

> The Fourth Armored Division is both feared and hated by German front line troops because of its high combat efficiency. Some American prisoners of war who could speak and understand German were told by enemy soldiers and officers that the Fourth Armored Division has gained a reputation amongst the Wehrmacht of being a crack armored unit dangerous to oppose.

And it was about this time the Germans picked up the nickname "Tiger Jack" for General Wood and Goebbels started railing against the 4th Armored Division's "butchers."

And so it was ironic that on 3 December, just as the 4th Armored Divsion had consolidated its positions around Domfesel and was ready to drive on to new glories, that the division and the leader, who had done so much to make and shape it into the superlative fighting instrument it had become, were separated. "Tiger Jack" was relieved and sent home to rest with words of praise ringing in his ears, and assurances by both Patton and Eisenhower that they wanted him back as soon as possible for an even higher command.

They said they wanted me to get a rest from combat and wanted me back as soon as I had got it. I told them they were wrong, that all I wanted was to remain with my division, but that as a soldier I would carry out the orders. I think they were sincere in their expressions of concern. George Patton I loved like a brother and Eisenhower I had liked since my first sight of him when he reported as a "beast," or new cadet, to "P" Company in 1911 where I was in charge of "beast barracks" and responsible for the induction of new cadets into the Corps. Both were sincere, but I think they knew they were only sugar-coating a very bitter pill.

So ended my active participation in battle. My only consolation was that my Division went on to further glories under two successive commanders in the few remaining months of the war in Europe, with no change in its methods or its indomitable spirit. Many of my officers and men wrote me after I left saying that they were carrying on as I had taught them and that though there were other commanders assigned to them, there was never any other leader. Their affection and their confidence in me has lasted through the years, and in it I take great pride beyond all telling.

The full story of Wood's relief has never been told, but it was no secret in the 4th Armored Division that Wood and Major General Manton S. Eddy, commanding the XII Corps, were, at times, uneasy bedfellows. Both of them were superior generals, but in quite different ways. Wood was volatile, impatient, never a "yes man"; not a submissive subordinate.

On the Army list Wood was senior to most of the commanders in Europe, and he had been both critical and correct — two attributes which did not win friends or influence people.

He had seen—and emphasized—missed opportunities, in Brittany and again near Sarrebourg in September. By 1 December Wood, like his division, was tired, irritable, emotional, tense, and frustrated by what he considered unnecessary bloodshed caused by the stupidity of higher-ups. His troops, with approval of higher command echelons, had crossed the Third Army boundary into the Seventh Army zone, and had become involved, in the last days of November, in the dog-fight with the Panzer Lehr Division, remaining in The Seventh Army area considerably longer than General Eddy had expected. In the later words of Brigadier General Hal C. Pattison, one of the key officers of the 4th Armored in these actions was

> ... mal-assigned as a commander ... his bent was mechanical engineering, his talent was research and development. He was a grand gentleman and a perfect host. He was not a troop leader and, especially he was not a tank unit commander. It seemed that everyone in the Division except General Wood knew ... [his] failings. Wood's one great weakness was his almost blind loyalty to "my people." We could do no wrong.

The explosion that took place in the 4th Armored Division's command post in or near a railroad station near Macwiller, on or about the 1st or 2nd of December, was thus touched off by a long, long fuse, indeed—clashing personalities, old animosities and frictions, and a whole host of aggravations, large and small.

Pattison witnessed what happened between Manton Eddy and John Shirley Wood, both of them aggressive and top-notch commanders, but with utterly discrepant personalities.

> ... there was an immediate and angry exchange; in retrospect it seemed to be a continuation of an earlier argument. General Eddy said the Division was not fighting hard, was not living up to its capabilities and would have to move faster. General Wood angrily disputed these charges and Eddy retorted that he, Wood, had promised to be out of the Seventh Army zone in a couple of days

and it still was blocking the 44th Division's roads after more than a week . . . . To which General Wood, who rarely swore, replied "God damn it, Matt, my boys have bought every foot of this ground with their blood, they have done everything humanly possible and I will not ask any more of them. We will get out as fast as we can but no faster!"...General Wood then turned on his heel and stalked out leaving a very angry General Eddy behind him . . . . Eddy must have asked Patton to relieve his friend Wood [whom he, Eddy, respected] from command of his division. The relief came on 3 December.

This clash of two strong-willed men might, it appears in retrospect, have been avoided. There was fault on both sides. Wood's failing was his almost "blind loyalty" to a subordinate commander who should have been relieved; Eddy's to charge the 4th Armored with their record of accomplishment, with a lack of combat aggressiveness and with blocking the 44th Division's roads needlessly—a charge which, in retrospect, this division, heavily engaged with the Panzer Lehr attack, did not deserve.

Nevertheless, the deed was done. The Army's official history—"The Lorraine Campaign" (H. M. Cole)—sums up the relief as follows:

On 3 December Major General Hugh J. Gaffey relinquished his post as the Third Army Chief of Staff to Brigadier General Hobart R. Gay and relieved Major General John S. Wood who had commanded the 4th Armored Division in the successful campaign across France and during the heartbreaking actions in the autumn mud. Wood, a brave and energetic commander, had been affected by the strain of battle, like so many of his officers and men. Fatigued as he was, Wood could no longer carry the burden of his command. General Patton and General Eddy reluctantly concluded that he would have to go back to the United States for a rest. The 4th Armored Division itself was badly in need of rest and reorganization. Continuous fighting, under conditions which prewar field manuals had taught were impossible for armor, had seriously reduced its tank complement and induced severe losses among its experienced combat personnel — particularly officers . . .

Wood was tired and tense; in combat he gave all of himself, and General Gay wrote to the author, in a letter of February, 1967:

> Wood was not relieved of command of the 4th Armored Division for so-called cause. He was relieved because of health. He was a *sick* man and so pronounced by all medical officers concerned, viz, Corps, Army and Army Group. It was Patton's definite understanding and he so informed "P" that he was being sent home for a long deserved rest and to fit him physically for a higher command.*

After General Wood's death, Eisenhower wrote to Mrs. Wood:

> "P" came to see me personally before he left [France], still anxious to stay with his division. Of course none of us at that time knew what the duration of the war would be and my personal concern was to get "P" back in shape to take over either his own Division or a Corps. His reputation as a fighting man was unexcelled and he urged me to over-ride the doctors and send him back to his original post of duty . . . .

A year or so before his death Wood himself told friends that after his relief he had stopped at "Ike's Headquarters" and had been assured by General Walter Bedell Smith — Eisenhower's Chief of Staff — that Eisenhower agreed Wood was to come back to command of the 4th Armored after a month or six weeks rest in the States. Patton, too, wanted "him back."

But it was not to be. After a month's rest in the United States, Wood reported to General George C. Marshall, Army Chief of Staff in Washington, who told him he was, in Hal

---

*Gay became Patton's Chief of Staff of the Third Army, when Major General Hugh Gaffey relieved Wood.

Pattison's words, "needed more at Fort Knox [Kentucky] commanding the Armored Force Center and training the Armor officers and men for reinforcements than commanding a division in Europe."

Wood himself speculated later about the reasons for his relief; he rejected the medical verdict that he was worn out in combat and wrote in his memoirs:

> I suppose I will never know the entire story behind the withdrawal from combat of a division commander who was acknowledged to have achieved outstanding and unprecedented success in the employment of armor. Perhaps I had been too outspoken in my criticism of the static minds and rigid conceptions of the high command in Brittany . . . . And perhaps I had been too emphatic in my protests against linear employment of our forces, particularly armor, in frontal attacks all along the front instead of in deep thrusts in decisive directions."

The clearest insight into the circumstances surrounding General Wood's relief—at the very apex of his fame—has been furnished by Brigadier General Hal Pattison, who served throughout the war with the 4th Armored, witnessed the encounter between Eddy and Wood, and later was the Chief of Military History of the Army. In a lengthy letter to Michael R. Peed of the University of Arizona,* General Pattison sums up the circumstances of this Greek tragedy.

Wood, he notes, "was inclined to be headstrong and independent." Bruce C. Clarke, who was Chief of Staff of the 4th Armored under General Wood for more than a year, and then, until 1 November 1944, was Commanding Officer of Combat Command A,* was an excellent foil for Wood's dynamism. Clarke was a pragmatist; Wood "leaned heavily"

---

*1971, copies on file in the Office of Military History.

---

*He was promoted to Brigadier General and transferred to the 7th Armored Division.

upon Clarke's counsel, which served as a "steadying influence on Wood's sometime volatile temperament."

. . . With the departure of Clarke there was no one left, in a position to do so, who either could or would restrain his [Wood's] impetuosity . . . . Wood was a hard man to handle and he made enemies. There is no doubt . . . that he was emotionally drained at that period. For the first time since entering combat his "people" were suffering heavy casualties and he felt frustrated at the restrictions terrain, weather and men were placing upon his beloved 4th Armored Division...

John Shirley Wood was not an easy subordinate. He was a highly intelligent and perceptive man who did not "suffer fools gladly" no matter what their station. He was, in fact, openly contemptuous of men he considered to be of lesser competence and had, for example, tangled publicly with General Ben Lear in Tennessee and General [Walton] Walker* when he thought they were grossly in error. On the other hand he was a matchless leader who inspired trust, confidence and love in his subordinates down to the last private in the Division. To this day he is a legend to the veterans of the 4th Armored Division and to them he is still The Division Commander.

Wood shared the hardships and the triumphs of his men, and on the scales of military history his accomplishments gave honest measure. He did much at the least possible cost in the blood of his men; what roused him to fury were stupidities and mistakes which caused needless casualties.

And so a great collaboration ended—one of the most successful in the history of warfare—between a leader and the led, between a great division commander and a division that carved its fighting name across the heart of Europe.

The division was to go on to new glories and to compile a record unsurpassed—in fact rarely equalled—in results achieved as compared to casualties taken, in combat effective-

---

*Then commanding general, XX Corps, Third Army, and a classmate of Wood's at West Point.

ness, in aggressiveness, in mobility, in teamwork, and professionalism, in all that makes a division great. No one unit in, or attached to, the division, had a monopoly of effectiveness; somehow "P" Wood's spirit was infused into them all. The self-propelled automatic weapons AA Battalion, for instance, established an ETO (European Theatre of Operations) record of 35 German planes destroyed in one 24-hour period, and a campaign record of a total of 134 enemy aircraft downed in ten months of fighting.

Three Medals of Honor, 4,000 decorations, more than 90,000 German prisoners, almost 14,000 enemy dead, a Presidential Citation, at a cost of 1,519 officers and men killed in action—these are some of the accolades, some of the grim statistics of victory that history records.

Many of the 4th did not live to see the battle streamers of France and Lorraine and the Bulge and Germany added to the division's colors; the sergeant who had coined a battle cry at Avranches—"They've got us surrounded again, the poor bastards"—died in Germany just beyond the Siegfried Line. But the Division and "Tiger Jack," the man who more than any other single individual gave it its soul, though separated physically, were inseparable in spirit then and now.

★ THE GENERAL ★

IN THE U.S. ARMY THE 1930'S WAS A PERIOD OF GESTA-
tion; the ideas, the weapons, the tactics that were to win
World War II were being slowly developed.

A few men played key roles; "P" Wood was one of them.

Wood studied and rejected the concept of static positions—
the Maginot Line mentality—as early as 1931, after he com-
pleted his course at the Ecole de Guerre. He wrote, in a report to the War Department, that "if we had to base our
future development on foreign ideas, we should take those of
people like Von Seeckt," the father of the renascent German
Army, rather than the defensive conceptions of the French.
He read de Gaulle, Fuller and Liddell Hart, and became an
early convert to the belief that "the next war would be one
of rapid movement, of motors, tanks and aviation, of indirect
approach and deep penetrations, regardless of flank protection and linear formations."

But "the going was hard for new ideas." The "innova-
tors"—as in most armies except the German—"were sub-
merged by the mass of static military thought."

In the United States Army in 1935, while the theory of
Blitzkrieg was in gestation in Germany, armor was conspicuous by its absence. At Pine Camp, New York, in August,

103

1935, during the climax of the largest peacetime maneuvers the United States Army had ever held, two tanks, about *one-third* of the total number of *serviceable* modern tanks then available to the entire Army, made an inauspicious appearance before high-ranking officers and foreign military attaches. One tank had a mechanical breakdown and was stranded within "enemy" lines; the second "bellied up" on a stump, its tracks moving aimlessly like the feet of a turtle in mid-air.

The prophets of the future form of war were without honor in their own country.

But Wood persisted. He was considered foolish by his friends in 1936 when he turned down an Army War College assignment and "welcomed the chance to command the Army's only independent truck-drawn howitzer organization in Des Moines, Iowa."

Ft. Des Moines, Iowa, 1937. Lt. Col. Wood, at his desk as Commanding Officer, 80th Field Artillery Regiment, Motorized. (155mm Howitzer)

I was more interested in developing mechanization and armor . . . .

Under Wood the truck-drawn howitzers "developed methods of motor movement and control that were entirely new in the service, travelling thousands of miles across the country to different firing points."

This experience and command of a motorized artillery brigade enabled Wood to try out the ideas of mobility, movement and fire power he had read about and discussed.

But the old horsed cavalrymen too often opposed the new iron steeds. Major General John K. Herr, Chief of Cavalry, asked "P" Wood in 1940, as he was reporting as George Patton's artillery commander in the 2nd Armored Division, "Are you going down to join that bunch of starry-eyed s.o.b.'s?"

The infantry was still the self-proclaimed Queen of Battles, and the linear theories of World War I were still doctrine at the Army Command and General Staff School at Leavenworth on the eve of World War II. Only the efforts of a few true believers, "farsighted leaders like Adna Chaffee, Bruce Palmer, Sr., Charles L. Scott and 'Jake' Devers," prepared the United States Army for the mechanized war of movement that was impending.

Hitler's rise in Germany and the development of the phobic militaristic-chauvinism of Japan meant to all perceptive men the inevitability of conflict. The incentive of history and an urgency of purpose were now helping that small band of professionals who were trying to prepare the Army for the greatest war of all time.

Wood believed that mobility—the plane-tank team, the basic building block of what came to be known as *Blitzkrieg*— was the key to the impending conflict. He had little patience with those who looked backwards; fire power and mobility were his credo, "book" solutions his bane. Years afterwards he remembered, somewhat sardonically, the 1939 Louisiana Maneuvers, first of a series of large-scale exercises in which the U.S. Army grew to tactical maturity. These maneuvers had, as a major objective, the "determination of whether the 75 mm gun or the 105 howitzer should be the basic weapon for field artillery."

Wood, as chief of staff to the maneuver director, had already made up his mind; the 75 was a great weapon of yesterday; the 105 was the weapon of today.

> I wrote the report in favor of the howitzer before the maneuvers began, and it was duly incorporated in the final report.

Wood was ahead of his time. In reports to the Chief of Field Artillery and in articles written for the *Field Artillery Journal* during 1938-1939 he pin-pointed the need for:

1. The 105 mm as standard direct support artillery.
2. The 105 mm and the 155 mm as divisional artillery.
3. The 8 inch and the 155 mm as Army and General Support artillery.
4. The 105 mm and 75 mm as self-propelled artillery for armored units.
5. Improved aerial observation for artillery, and ground units of all types.
6. Large scale motor movements.

In a March 25, 1939, paper addressed to the Chief of Field Artillery when Wood was still a lieutenant-colonel, he wrote, in his opening paragraph, that,

> ... the recommendations of the caliber board for the artillery armament of the United States Army are generally out of date, and it is doubtful if the ideals set up by this board were even correct at the time of its publication [in May 1919] ....The progress in mechanical transportation, mechanized weapons, and aviation has materially changed many of the bases for the recommendations of the board .... army weapons ... should be as mobile as possible .... the modernization of our artillery weapons are meaningless unless accompanied by plans for the simultaneous or prior development of proper air observation.

In the *Field Artillery Journal* (May-June 1939), he wrote "the motor offers one of the few hopes of securing surprise in modern war."

This kind of prescience—like Wood's capability for judging his friends objectively—was sometimes irritating, often all the more so because his judgements were usually correct.

The development of armor in the United States was slow, despite the crusading spirit of a handful of officers, and the theoretical groundwork laid by men like Adna Chaffee and Charles L. Scott.

Even in the Plattsburgh Maneuvers of 1939 armor was still in swaddling clothes in the U.S. Army. Tanks were still called "combat cars," the nomenclature of the cavalry. The nation's only major tank unit, the thin beginnings of the great sixteen division armored force of World War II, was a single brigade—the Seventh Cavalry Brigade (Mechanized)— which had to share its glory during the war games with a horsed cavalry regiment. The tanks, though called by another name, were conceded grudgingly in the critique to be a "powerful arm and a great asset," though one with many limitations.

The Brigade, following the maneuvers, marched to New York City with its 650 vehicles including 112 "combat cars" or light tanks, and, en route to the World's Fair, paraded

1939; one of the U.S. Army's early tanks, or "Combat Cars" as they were called then—the old twin-turret "Mae West" light tank.

through the city to the acclaim of New Yorkers, who, impressed by the clanking tanks, mistook a spectacle for national strength. Ironically, the Brigade, the principal armored force of the U.S. Army, arrived at the Fair in Flushing Meadows, the so-called "World of Tomorrow" on 31 August, 1939, just as Hitler's legions, with thousands of tanks and planes, commenced their conquest of Europe with the invasion of Poland.

Even after the war started, resistance to armor continued. The Polish campaign, the detractors held, was fluke; the Poles offered no worthwhile opposition. The proper way to use tanks was to support infantry, not to group them together in large and cumbersome armored units.

Wood, as a lieutenant-colonel, became chief of staff of the Third Army at Atlanta, Georgia, as the great war started in September 1939. He was promoted to colonel and in April 1941, was assigned as artillery commander of the 2nd Armored Division, under George Patton, at Fort Benning, Georgia. By then, France had been crushed under the juggernaut of the German plane-tank team, and the Nazi Blitzkrieg tactics had overrun an army that had been called "the best in the world" and could no longer be denied.

Yet the resistance to change, the struggle to maintain the pre-eminence of the old arms—particularly of the infantry—prevented a straight-line development of armor. The nation's armored strength made progress like a frog leaping out of a well—three leaps upwards, two back.

The fall of France and the German conquest of all of Europe unquestionably spurred the organization of tanks into armored divisions; no longer were they merely parcelled out to support the infantry. Even so, a new "tank killer" was conjured up to defeat the tank; for a time, these so-called "tank destroyers"—mobile high-velocity guns on tracks without armor—were hailed as the conqueror of the tank, even before the United States tried them in battle or tested them in exercises. Wood and General Patton were told by General Lesley J. McNair, who was training the expanding Army, that it

... would be necessary to wait until the findings of

that year's [1940-1941] Louisiana Maneuvers to really know what tanks could do in the face of tank destroyer forces.

The only tank destroyers we had at that time were theoretical ones of scantlings mounted on jeeps, waiving yellow flags to indicate fire . . . .

The tankers—Patton, Scott, Wood and a handful of fiery converts—maintained that the best way to defeat the tank was with other tanks, and that armor should be grouped and organized into divisions and corps, each division with its own integral armored infantry units, the whole trained to fire and maneuver, speed and mobility. Their prognosis was to be sustained to a great degree by the lesson of combat.

Wood combined to a rare degree the qualities of a leader and man of action with those of the military intellectual. He wrote, thought, and pondered deeply about war in general and tactics in particular. In a lengthy and detailed contribution to the "Notes and Comments" section of the *Field Artillery Journal* for May-June 1939, he discussed French, German, Italian, and British tactical concepts and called for the creation of what later came to be the basic tactical building block of the U.S. Army, the task force of all arms,

> . . . trained in the combined action of all . . . elements, not as separate infantry, artillery, or other units thrown together by chance, but as essential parts of a single fighting organization . . . capable of rapid movement and rapid maneuver . . . .

The concept of grouping armor into special armored divisions, or task forces of all arms, was eventually "sold," despite the doubters.

The Armored Force was created with General Jacob L. Devers—a thoroughly professional soldier with a great gift of leadership and a contagious and persuasive personality—as its chief. General Devers, in General Wood's opinion, was "primarily responsible for the formation and equipment of the sixteen armored divisions that finally comprised" the force.

Wood did not remain long with the 2nd Armored; he was

109

already marked for higher command, and, in June of 1941, he became chief of staff of the nation's first armored corps under Major General Charles L. Scott. The armored corps, streamlined and tailored to direct masses of armor in a fast-moving battle, was doomed soon after its inception.

A corps organization of this sort for the employment of armored divisions would have been invaluable in France, but it met criticism and opposition in the War Department and all corps headquarters were made of the same type, no matter what sort of units they were to handle. Again static minds and service jealousies had prevailed.

On 31 October 1941, Wood was promoted to Brigadier General and was shortly assigned command of CC A of the 5th Armored Division in California. He reached the West Coast soon after Pearl Harbor:

> Rumors were rife of an impending invasion of the West Coast; black-outs were ordered; spies were seen every time a light flashed; Japanese submarines were on the prowl along the coast . . . airplanes over Los Angeles were met with fire from eager antiaircraft batteries; the War Department sent daily warnings to be ready . . . .
>
> I was ordered to take a task force of decrepit tanks, unfledged artillery, and untrained infantry to Los Angeles for repelling invaders along the 500 miles of coast from Oxnard to San Diego . . . . I established my headquarters in the Hollywood Race Track where I occupied *Whirlaway*'s stall, just vacated.
>
> Each day we sent our people to the beaches to fire precious ammunition in learning to pull lanyards, discharge rifles, and load machine guns, clamoring each night by letter and telegram for a few more rounds for real action.

Finally Wood was sent in person to see the general commanding the West Coast about the ammunition problem and discovered, to his horror, there "was no ammunition!"

"We were all much pleased," he later wrote drily, "when the Japanese Fleet was turned back at Midway."

110

Fort Benning, GA, September 1941. Brig. Gen. Wood, newly promoted, just prior to leaving to command CC "A" of the 5th Armored Division in California.

Pine Camp, N.Y. 1942. Maj. Gen. Wood reviews his command. In Front: Gen. Wood, CG 4th Armored Division; 2nd Row, l to r: Brig. Gen. Allen, CG CC "A", Col. Bruce Clarke, C/S, Brig. Gen. Dager, CG CC "B"; 3rd Row, Color Bearers.

On 15 April 1942, the 4th Armored Division was activated and in May 1942, the General and the Division met. Wood was shifted to command the 4th at Pine Camp, New York, and on 21 June 1942, he pinned the two silver stars of a Major General on his shoulders.

I took over from my friend [Major General] Henry Baird [who had organized the division] and found Bruce Clarke [later General], there as chief of the division staff. He had just been promoted to colonel from his job as commanding officer of the 24th Engineers. That began an association in training and fighting which, from my standpoint, could not have been bettered. Vernon Prichard and Rod Allen were my generals in charge of combat commands. They were outstanding and for that reason were soon promoted and sent on to organize and command other armored divisions. We supplied many thousands of men and officers, among them a dozen or more generals, as cadres for other divisions.

When my friend Holmes Dager, who became a great fighting leader of armor, was assigned to us as one of my combat commanders, he sent me a telegram wanting to know when he should report and asking for information as to what he should do about his wife and his household goods. I wired him, "ABANDON WIFE, STORE FURNITURE, AND REPORT AT ONCE." He understood and reported forthwith.

We trained and sent away many thousands from the 4th Armored Division. We tried to give the other divisions an even break in these transfers. We did not send the worst but we did not fail to keep the best. In this way we pared down to a tested lot of young fighting men with young officers and battalion commanders—leaders like Creighton Abrams, Hal Pattison, Delk Oden, John Sullivan, "Al" Irzyk, "Tom" Conley, "Art" West and DeWitt Smith, all of whom rose to general officer rank in the Army. Bruce Clarke went on from one high command to another, retiring as the Commander in Chief of our Army Forces in Europe. Creighton Abrams rose to four-star rank commanding U.S. Forces in Vietnam, and, ultimately,

Army Chief of Staff before his untimely death in 1974.

We trained in the snows of northern New York, along the streams and river crossings of East Tennessee, in the sands and great spaces of our western desert, in the brush and heat of Texas, in the fields and downs and lanes of Wiltshire in England—and we arrived finally in the hedgerows of Normandy.

As soon as he assumed command, Wood immediately gave the division his own restless pride, his high standards, his aggressiveness, and his sense of innovation. He would try anything once; he encouraged initiative. The division did a "lot of experimenting" in the summer of 1942; Wood had "ideas and was willing to give them without reserve."

His disciplinary ideas were, to most in the Army, novel. He was a stickler for high standards. Despite the heat of the Desert Training Center in California where the 4th Armored was sent in the fall of 1942,

General Wood had an inviolate rule that the fatigue clothes which we wore all the time would be buttoned to the last button at the collar and the sleeves rolled down at all times.

He enforced this religiously throughout the division. He made it stick. No one liked it.

But he was not a martinet, or a "spit-and-polish" general. He believed the military salute was a soldier's greeting—as indeed it is—not merely a recognition of rank; thus, he saluted first, regardless of whom he met—private, cook, or colonel. Soon, the men of the Division were in a saluting competition, trying to salute their commanding general and other officers before they were saluted.

. . . soldiers got into the spirit of the thing, and they would try to salute the Division Commander as far as they could see him, always trying to beat him to the punch.

One day in Lorraine, a miserable cold, wet day and very muddy, I saw General Wood coming down a side road and, at the same time, a handful of soldiers were running across the muddy field, trying to get in his line

Pine Camp, N.Y. 4th Armored men in "chow" line during winter training. This training paid dividends during the Battle of The Bulge in 1944-45.

Mojave Desert, 1943; Desert Training Center. Officers of 37th Tank Battalion during gunnery training (notice collars buttoned and sleeves rolled down). l to r; Lt. McMahon, Capt. Dwight, Lt. Scott, BN Surgeon.

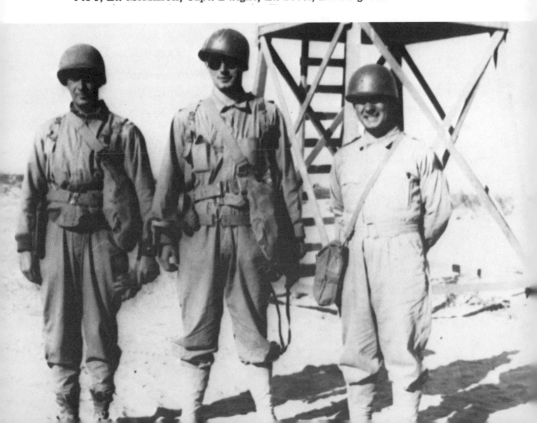

of sight so he'd see them salute. I think it had a lot to do with spirit.

Wood wouldn't accept "eight-balls," but, unlike most of the Army, he didn't transfer them to another outfit; he rehabilitated them. General Creighton Abrams recalled:

General Wood knew there would be misfits, an occasional inadequate, but he said: "Court-martials don't improve those few people—every one of them has a speck of gold somewhere in his heart. It's an officer's job to dig it up, and build on it! NO courts-martial!"

On officers, Wood was tough, but just as gentle, too. One mistake, maybe two was OK, but *never* the same one, and *never* in action! He believed and drilled into his leaders from non-coms up to the top, an appreciation of their responsibilities to their men. "You may have only eight, or even thousands of men in your unit, but always remember—each one has a Mother, Father, perhaps a wife and children. They want that soldier home, after this War ends! So you *invest* them carefully—*lead* them, don't just order them! Reconnoiter, see, estimate, *what* you are taking them into, weigh every advantage and disadvantage of your plan, attack fast and hard, pound out a win and come out of it with 90% of your people and equipment! Less than that—you are only a brass-buttoned figurehead!"

General Wood had a policy that began at Pine Camp where he just would not approve general courts-martial with sentences of confinement. That is, he would not approve the execution, but all of these sentences he would suspend the confinement and the dishonorable discharge and the soldier would be returned to duty. In the 24th Engineer Battalion there was a problem soldier who had been a problem for some length of time, and finally he misappropriated a government vehicle and got into an accident in which some people were injured. For about the fifth or sixth time, his battalion commander preferred charges against him, and he was tried by a general courts-martial and sentenced to a substantial confinement and a dishonorable discharge. As was his habit, the Division Commander, who was the reviewing authority, suspended the confinement and the dishonorable discharge. Whereupon, the battalion commander of the Engineer Battalion protested vigorously.

In the conference that took place between the Division Commander and the battalion commander, the Division Commander agreed that he would take the soldier and assign him himself. He took him as the Division Commander's driver.

Later on in England, elements of the Division were on an exercise and the Division Commander was out watching it, riding around in his jeep with this self-same driver that he had acquired at Pine Camp. During the course of the day, the jeep got in a difficult situation and overturned, throwing General Wood out and injuring his back, for which he was hospitalized for a short time. The driver actually came out of the accident unharmed, but was in such an emotional state because he felt that he had been responsible for hurting the Division Commander that it was required to keep him under sedation in the hospital for several days until he had achieved a better emotional balance.

Later on, one dark night in France, I remember being called to the division CP to see the Division Commander. After reporting to the Chief of Staff, I was directed to the Division Commander's tent. General Wood habitually lived in a small CP tent, which had a canvas covered passageway through which you entered it. It was a standard issue CP tent for the battalion headquarters and the like. It was very dark and I had located the tent and was making my way in this little passageway when someone stuck a Thompson submachine gun in my stomach, almost to the backbone. It was the same driver acquired at Pine Camp and still driving General Wood. I found out later that every night when General Wood was there this fellow slept on some straw in the little passageway.

The personal bond between General Wood and the men he commanded was compounded of many things — most of all

116

loyalty down and human warmth. Abrams also remembered that,

Up at division headquarters the division headquarters soldiers customarily had calisthenics at reveille. They had a cleared space that was not far from the Division Commander's tent in which he slept and lived, and each morning as the soldiers were there taking their calisthenics the Division Commander would come out and take a few exercises in front of his tent in a pair of trunks or some such clothing, at the end of which he would take a five-gallon can of water setting close at hand, open it and up-end it over his head, the water pouring down over him and so on, after which he would rub vigorously and then retire to his tent. The soldiers marvelled at this because some of these mornings were quite brisk, and they felt it was quite a performance. One morning the Division Commander did as he usually did, except when he up-ended the can and the water poured down over him, he let out a bloodcurdling and spontaneous yell. It turned out later that his orderly had neglected to preheat the water. I have heard soldiers and officers tell this story over and over again with a great deal of affection.

From the desert training center we went to Camp Bowie. This was in a dry belt of Texas and liquor was not for sale. General Wood authorized beer to be sold on the post in the post exchanges for soldiers. A great cry went up from the community of Brownwood. Pastors spoke from the pulpit against this practice and policy of General Wood's. Letters went to Congressmen and other officials appealing the decision of General Wood. Against all of these efforts, General Wood stood fast, saying that his soldiers had to have beer if they wanted it. Beer stayed in the post exchanges all the time that the 4th Armored Division was at Camp Bowie.

General Wood had a practice of coming around and speaking to battalion or even smaller groups of soldiers. This was generally a pre-planned affair and very simple. The soldiers would be assembled in formation and General Wood would drive up and get out of his jeep and walk out and would begin by asking all the soldiers to gather around him. And then he would talk to them and tell them how happy he was to see how well they looked, how healthy they were, how well their clothes looked, and he would congratulate them on the fine work that they were doing. And the talk would continue for five or ten minutes in this vein, and that would be the Division Commander's talk. He did this many, many times, both in the United States and in England and on the Continent, and his talk never varied very much, the words were always about the same. And so it wasn't too long before the men knew that General Wood was coming to talk to them, you would hear them talking among themselves and they would be reciting in advance what the Division Commander was going to tell them, and they were, of course, almost verbatim correct about what finally turned out to be his talk. They loved to do this, not in a critical way or in a mimicking way, but they knew him and they knew what he was going to say, and they contemplated this with affection and good feeling.

The division experimented, trained, and drilled exhaustively, particularly with small unit tactics throughout 1942 and 1943. Essentially, Wood's formula was speed and drive— "vicious, smashing action," to "hit fast and hard."

Simplicity in planning and particularly in operational orders were stressed; oral rather than written instructions were emphasized. The tanks learned all the tricks of fire and maneuver. Unlike most of the other armored divisions, they practiced moving fire, learning to lay effectively their guns and fire on the move to compensate for the roll and pitch of the lumbering monsters. Flank attack against the more vulnerable sides and tracks of the enemy was practiced; the armored infantry was trained to accompany and support the tanks; the guns rolled along in direct support. At the Desert Training Center, the armored charge—tanks and half-tracks in widely deployed formation, accelerators jammed to the floor, guns blazing—was tested.

It was during this period of training for the great adven-

Tennessee Maneuvers - October 1942. Men in half track; Company C, 37th Tank Battalion; l to r; Sgt. Harler, Commo. Sgt., and PFC Budnick.

ture that Wood clinched his hold forever upon the affections of the 4th Armored Division, and, in doing it, almost lost his official head before he ever saw action.

The division was sent to the Tennessee Army Maneuvers from early September to mid-November 1942, where new divisions were being trained and whipped into shape by a flinty disciplinarian, Lieutenant General Ben Lear, commanding the 2nd Army. Lear, an old cavalryman of redoubtable phlegm, was the kind of officer every army needs — but not too many of them. He was a good, though unimaginative, trainer, but no man for innovation. He lived by the book, ruled by fear and had little use for the new-fangled iron steeds.

Lear had laid down a rigid schedule of weekly maneuvers; inflexible rules and umpire judgments were supposed to make them last a full three days at minimum.

119

Wood had little use for the artificialities of controlled maneuvers; fortunately for him, General Jacob L. Devers, who had just been assigned in 1942 to command the Armored Force, felt as he did. Later, Devers wrote:

> This force was falling off a pedestal set high by Major Daniel Van Voorhis, and the task of organizing and training was most difficult. There were no tanks worthy of the name, no firepower, no self-propelled artillery, no proper design for track propulsion, and, worst of all, no tank engines with adequate horse power . . . .

> The Army Ground Forces had set up a system of weights based on firepower for the use of umpires in deciding who was the victor [in maneuvers]. These weights were not realistic as applied to the armored divisions. I consulted with General [George C.] Marshall, [Army Chief of Staff] and asked him whether, in a maneuver, the commander who took full advantage of the rules and regulations in a ruthless manner and brought it to an end in a short time would be considered correct. He replied that he always did that himself. I consulted with "P" Wood, and asked him what his manuever was going to be. He had the idea of the modern football coach of opening up a hole with firepower, shooting a fast unit through the opening at great speed with blockers proctecting on all sides. I told him to intensify this effort and make it work, and we alerted the umpires to use their mathematical formulas on the use of firepower so that we would not be held up by referees calling clipping, and stopping the maneuver. Thus the 4th Armored did under "P's" leadership, and the commanding general was furious. I was present at his critique and defended "P" so that we managed to get our point across. This was the beginning of a great up-surge of respect for the armored units.

But this successful development of the armored tactics of firepower, shock, and mobility probably made less of an impression on the 4th Armored Division than did General Wood's fiery public defense of his division against what he felt to be unjust criticism from General Lear. Indeed, the

Old "Fuss-budget" himself: Lt. Gen. Lear inspecting company kitchen. (Note: no photos of Lear-Wood incident were made.)

Lear-Wood incident has rarely been equalled in the recorded history of armies. Eyewitnesses have described it in different ways. Brigadier General Hal C. Pattison, in recalling the incident, states that,

> ... the 4th Armored Division was showing its tendency for the bold and the unorthodox [during the Tennessee maneuvers] and as a result drew down upon itself frowns of disapproval from General Lear and the 2d Army staff. About midway through the period, General Lear was called to Washington to be gone for a period of three days. He was to depart on a Sunday night and return late on Wednesday. The critiques of the weekly maneuvers were normally held on Sunday morning, following completion of the maneuver and the assembly of the units in preparation for the next problem. In the critique held on the Sunday morning before his departure, General Lear expressed himself in no uncertain terms about the propensity of the 4th Armored Division to move and operate

under the cover of darkness, and the inability of umpires to restrain the division in order to drag the maneuver problems out to their planned duration. He stated in no uncertain terms that the problem scheduled to be held during his absence was to go for a minimum of three days, or the responsible individuals would suffer dire consequences.

The maneuver held during that particular week was the defense of the river line forward of the river. An Infantry division was on the defense, the 4th Armored Division was attacking. By noon of the first day, Monday, the umpires had had to employ a number of artificial decisions in order to slow up the attacking force. The division reserve, a light tank battalion, had with it only its battalion umpire who was a relatively young and inexperienced officer. The division was held up by the chief umpire. General Wood directed his reserve tank battalion [then commanded by Lieutenant Colonel Hal C. Pattison] to attack along the woods road which constituted the boundary between two regiments of the defending force.

The battalion was directed to go to its attack position late in the afternoon and to launch its attack about thirty minutes before dark. Without describing the details of the attack, it is sufficent to state that this battalion overran the headquarters of the infantry regiment in the line, the reserve regiment, and some of the positions of the division artillery, overran the bivouac of the tank battalion of the defending force, captured both bridges of the defending force across the river, desroying one, and at daylight of Tuesday, was firmly established in a bridgehead of its own on the remaining bridge. Needless to say, regardless of action the umpires took, the maneuver was over.

At the critique the following Sunday, General Lear was beside himself with anger. He castigated General Wood and his division in no uncertain terms, criticizing them severely for employing tactics and techniques which were completely impracticable for armor to employ, for violating the plans of war and for being guilty of poor judgment, to say nothing of being an undisciplined rabble.

As the officers of the division listened with rising anger, they did not observe the effect this criticism was having on General Wood until he charged onto the platform, interrupting General Lear to tell him in the most positive tone and words that he [Lear] did not know what he was talking about either as to the employment of armor or the quality of the people of his division. General Lear ordered General Wood off the platform, but he refused to go until Colonel Bruce Clarke, his Chief of Staff, fearful of what this exchange might lead to, urged General Wood off the platform and out the back door where General Lear followed to continue the argument.

Word of this exchange spread rapidly throughout the division, and from that day forward, every man knew that General Wood would stand between them and blame.

Bruce Clarke, then division Chief of Staff, recorded, years afterwards, his vivid impressions of the incident:

Ben Lear usually spent an hour detailing horrible examples of how stupid squad and platoon leaders had acted as reported by his observers . . . .

"P" was boiling mad at this. Finally he could hold himself no longer. He asked Lear if he could talk and took the stage . . . . He said that he had sat through several of these Sunday sessions when he would be better off in church. He said he had listened to enough incidents of stupid sergeants and lieutenants. He said they were just learning. He felt we should talk about stupid generals who should have learned better.

Lear ordered him off the stage. He shook his finger [under] "P's" nose. I rushed on the stage, pushed between them, and led "P" to his car and we left for camp . . . .

From then on "P" was a great hero to his soldiers and young officers.

General Creighton Abrams, then a tank battalion commander in the 4th, remembered the same or a somewhat similar incident, in slightly different terms:

> ... on the Tennessee maneuvers the practice was to maneuver through the week and complete it on Friday, and then on Saturday morning there would always be a meeting in a ... school auditorium in Lebanon, at which various members of the directing staff and some commanders would make comments, and always winding up with the final comment on the week's activities by General Lear who was the commander and director of these maneuvers. During one week, the 4th Armored Division made a night river crossing of the Cumberland River. My battalion, a tank battalion, when its initial elements were crossing over this Engineer-constructed floating bridge, the bridge broke, and three tanks dropped into some 50 feet of water in the Cumberland River. Unfortunately, seven men drowned as a result of this accident. At any rate, the following Saturday the critique as usual was going on at the high school auditorium in Lebanon, and we commanders were all present for the critique. At the end, General Lear rose and was addressing his remarks on the maneuver, and he came eventually to the point where he was critical of the professionalism of noncommissioned officers and junior officers.

> At midway in these remarks, General Wood turned and addressed himself to the group in the auditorium, explaining that he was proud of the way that the noncommissioned officers and junior officers were performing their jobs; as he thought they were the finest that the Army had ever had, and he said that if one really wanted to know them, then one had to be out with them in the woods and at night, and talk with them and watch what they actually did, and then one could be in a position to judge them with validity.

> Then he went on to say, "Seven soldiers of the 4th Armored Division lost their lives this week in an accident when the bridge broke over the Cumberland River," and he said, "These soldiers as surely gave their lives for their

124

country as if a Boche had shot them dead."

With this, he came to full attention and said, "I now give them their last salute." He executed a righthand salute. At that instant, as if a string was attached to everyone in the audience, they rose simultaneously, executed the righthand salute and stood silently at attention, saluting with General Wood. After a full minute or so, General Wood said, "Two," with which he and the others came down with the salute. General Wood vaulted off the stage and took his place at his seat. There was silence in the auditorium.

A staff officer of the headquarters said, "Dismissed," and with that, everyone filed out. General Wood assembled his commanders around him outside the auditorium and told them that he was proud of what everyone was doing; he wanted the word to be carried back to the men that he was proud of what they were doing and that he thought they were a splendid group. We returned by our various routes to our units, and I must say that we were somewhat saddened by this whole thing, because we felt surely that we would lose our division commander for what he had done. Right as he might be, nevertheless, what he had done was an unheard of thing in the Army. Of course, we didn't lose him, and word spread throughout the division about what had happened.

Colonel Arthur P. Nesbit, AUS, Retired, of Columbia, Tennessee, also remembered this incident and the impression it made on him:

There had been an accident, involving several tanks crossing the Cumberland river on a pontoon bridge, and several soldiers lost their lives in the accident. I recall that at the end of that phase a critique was held in some school house, and that General Ben Lear was to attend and possibly have some comment to make during the course of the critique. The atmosphere concerning that officer was as if the announcement were to be made that Almighty God were to arrive and for some reason, I cannot recall at the time, this particular accident was a thing which he seemed to have taken umbrage at. At that time and place, and in the light of the existing feeling of awe, fear, and dread which existed on the part of those subject to General Lear's authority, what General Wood did stands out in my mind as the bravest and most courageous act I have ever observed. He stood before the assembled officers, and most of them were relatively senior, eulogized those lads whose lives had been lost, said what should have been said; stated that they had given their lives for their country just as if they had fallen in battle, and saluted them as he finished. I recall that the reaction on the part of those who were there was tremendous, but it was a silent reaction since they did not have the temerity to join audibly in such tribute as I am sure they did in spirit.

This was the greatest act of cold courage I have ever observed or have known of (and also the finest act of *loyalty* from the top down imaginable, and that is where loyalty in any military organization has its genesis). This man, General John Shirley Wood, whom I had never seen before, and never had the privilege of seeing again, had actually put his career in the United States Army on the line when he paid tribute to those soldiers of his command and did what only a very great man would have wanted to do in the first place.

I was there with one Colonel Roger Williams, IGD, and we were from the Office of the Inspector General. Colonel Williams, after we left that auditorium, said that we had seen and listened to one real leader.

The incident in Tennessee dramatized Wood's tremendous strength and his one major failing. He had an intense, indeed fierce, sense of loyalty down; he was ready to act as shock absorber for all who served under him. But he had little toleration for rigidity, inflexibility, or stupidity and he could not condone it, even in his superiors; he felt his highest loyalty up was to his country and the Army he served, not to any single individual—even one of superior rank. He was, for many like Ben Lear, "obstreperous, hard to handle, a difficult subordinate," and he was never mealy-mouthed when he

126

Chippenham, England, 1944. Maj. Gen. Wood and his subordinate commanders. Left to right: Col. Bill Withers, Brig. Gen. Holmes Dager, Maj. Gen. John S. Wood, Col. Bixby, Col. Bruce C. Clarke.

Gen. Wood and 4th Armored Division Staff at Greenways Manor House, Chippenham, England, Spring 1944. Front Row, l to r: LTC John H. Hamelick, Adj: Gen; LTC Herbert F. Krucker, G-4; LTC Harry E. Brown, G-2; Col. Walter A. Bigby, C/S; Maj. Gen. Wood; Col. Wendell Blanchard, C.O. Div. Trains; LTC John B. Sullivan, G-3; LTC Robert M. Connolly, G-1; LTC Otto T. Saar, Signal. O. Back Row, l to r: LTC Emmet P. Crane, Div. Chaplain; Capt. (unidentified) Asst. Ordanance O; LTC Carlos Reynolds, C.O. 126 Ordance BN & Div. Ordanance O; LTC Morris Abrams, Div. Surgeon; LTC Clarence O. Brunner, Inspector General; LTC Lawrence F. Dorato, Div. Chemical Officer; Maj. (unidentified) Div. Ammo O; LTC James VanWagener, G-5; LTC Louis E. Roth, CO 24th Engr Bn & Div Engineers; LTC Harold E. Miller, Div Quarter Master, LTC Chester D. Silvers, Judge Advocate General.

4th A.D. HQ in England at Chippenham. Maj. Gen. Wood confers with British officers and his Signal Officer Lt. Col. Saar.

felt his superiors were wrong. Once he was to tell Lieutenant General Walton H. Walker, who had been a classmate of Wood's at West Point and was then a corps commander, "Johnny; you never did have any sense; you always were a yearling corporal; you don't make any sense . . . ." (Walker was later killed while commanding the Eighth Army in Korea).

Nevertheless, the Tennessee Maneuvers represented a high point in the careers of both Wood and the 4th Armored Division; from then on, these two were forever mated, and earmarked for immortality. The life of the Division Commander and the corporate life of an inanimate unit, made viable by the men who manned it and the leader who led it, merged thereafter in the Desert Training Center; in the move overseas to England in December 1943 and January 1944; in the first half of 1944 during the unending training in England; and then, at last, in the trial by fire in France.

Wood and the 4th Armored were—and remain—one in that mystical union Guy Chapman has expressed so hauntingly in his World War I masterpiece, *A Passionate Prodigality*. Writing of his unit, the battalion with which he had served in the hell of trench warfare, he said:

> . . . this body of men had become so much part of me . . . [that] I was it, and it was I.

128

★ 6 ★

THE DIMENSIONS
OF LEADERSHIP

THE DIMENSIONS OF LEADERSHIP CANNOT BE DEFINED except in terms of personalities. One man's meat is another man's poison; the "Do's" of leadership for one general are the "Don'ts" for another. There are no inflexible rules or ineluctable truths; military leadership cannot be compressed into a textbook. It must be measured in terms of success or failure on the battlefield; in terms of the balance sheets of casualties suffered by the enemy versus losses sustained by our own; in terms of the hearts of men. In short, leadership is composed of a few constants and many variables; the variables are as diverse as Man. The best study of Mankind is Man.

Or, as General Wood put it in his memoirs:

... I do not believe it is possible to analyze the splendor of a sunset or to dissect the elements that make up the transcendent beauty of tracery and color in a butterfly's wing ... the command of troops in combat ... is ... the most difficult of arts, done with the lightest of touches.

Throughout history, there are few leaders and many led, and natural leadership, as distinct from generalship, is so rare that even in the military profession, which selects and breeds leaders, it is highly prized and avidly studied.

General Wood was a natural leader. Judged by any yardstick—the results he achieved, the reactions of the led, the evaluation of his peers and of history—he was one of the great division commanders of World War II, a leader exceptional even in the American Army.

Measured in terms of results achieved as compared to losses suffered or price paid, the 4th Armored Division was one of the great divisions of World War II; it probably exemplified the true role of armor—shock, fire power, momentum—better than any other division.

George Patton, under whom the 4th Armored Division served, described its accomplishments as "unequalled in the history of warfare." It led the breakout from Normandy and the great swinging pursuit across France to the Siegfried Line; it relieved Bastogne in the bloody Bulge battle and drove deep into Germany. Perhaps never has a division moved so far so fast and inflicted such discrepant losses on an enemy—14,000 enemy dead, 90,000 German prisoners, the Heartland of the enemy penetrated, at a cost of 1,519 men killed in action. And, even though Wood commanded the division in combat only about four months, from the breakout in Normandy to the Saar, it was *his* division—trained and shaped by him. "P" Wood's division was acknowledged by his successors, the late Hugh J. Gaffey and William M. Hoge, retired, as one of the finest fighting instruments in the American Army of World War II.

> Under General Wood, the 4th Armored Division set a style of fighting that characterized it throughout the war in Europe. It was daring, hard-riding, fast-shooting style.*

To the men he led to victory—and some to death—"P" Wood was a father-image, as well as a general, a natural leader,

---

*Armor Magazine, September-October 1966.

a man with a fierce, almost an obsessive, loyalty to those he led.

"They would follow him to hell today," General Jacob L. Devers, USA, Retired, said recently at West Point after General Wood was buried in the West Point cemetery.

Even in France men of the division hurried across the fields to salute their general, to see him and be seen by him.

Wood looked out for his men. Living much like his men, he slept under canvas, used a jerry can for a shower, and scorned the elaborate vans so many commanders used in France. When good food or captured German liquor was available, it was issued first to the tankers and the rifle squads, then on up the line.

A young rifle platoon commander in the 53rd Armored Infantry, now Major General DeWitt C. Smith, Jr., capsuled in a recent memo, the feelings of the men "P" Wood led. In referring to General Wood's relief as Division Commander, Smith wrote:

> I was not alone.
> ... [Wood was a] great, gusty, outgoing man ... with a tremendous sensitivity to human beings, a great love for his men, and a great faith in his Division. He was brave; had great moral courage; was outspoken; was warm and compassionate; could fight armor better than any man in Europe; had the ability to infuse high morale and *esprit* through convincing, personal leadership; and was beloved by us all for all of this. He was the finest soldier I have ever known and I shall never forget him.

Smith's appreciation, written more than twenty years later, cannot be dismissed as the hero worship of a young impressionable lieutenant for his division commander, for it is buttressed by the verdicts of Wood's peers and the appraisal of historians.

General Dwight D. Eisenhower regarded Wood as "a natural leader" from his cadet days, and "a splendid leader, a courageous and imaginative fighter."

Captain B.H. Liddell Hart, the British military historian and critic, has described Wood as "one of the most dynamic

133

commanders of armor in World War II and the first in the Allied Armies to demonstrate in Europe the essence of the art and tempo of handling a mobile force."

Chester Wilmot, the Australian historian, in his definitive history, *The Struggle for Europe,* describes Wood as a "bold, aggressive and original soldier," who, in fighting near Luneville, France, in September 1944, "handled his armor brilliantly..."

Major General F.W. von Mellenthin, the Chief of Staff of Germany Army Group G in the fighting in France in the fall of 1944, records a high respect for the general in his memoirs: "Wood of the 4th Armored proved himself an expert in armored tactics." There are, on record, other estimates of German respect.

General Paul Harkins, who was Patton's Deputy Chief of Staff in the Third Army, recalls Wood as a "grand leader of men."

The late General Creighton W. Abrams, Jr., Army Chief of Staff and United States Military Commander in Vietnam, who served under General Wood as commander of a tank battalion and a combat command, described Wood as "an inspirational leader, with the devotion of his people."

General Bruce C. Clarke, who won fame in command of CC A under Wood during the 4th Armored Division's dash across France, remembers Wood as a "strong character and a strong leader . . . ." In a philosophic vein, Clarke summed up, years later, the personal tragedy of a great soldier:

> The "Gods of War" did not smile on "P" Wood. He was older than the group in charge of the war in Europe. He was not an Infantryman. He was more brilliant in strategy than those above him and he let it be known. He served under Patton who was a showman and stole the headlines. "P" carried officers along who were incompetent, because they were "his boys."
>
> Under different circumstances "P" had the brains, the knowledge, the drive, the magnetic hold on his men to have been listed on the rolls of the "Great Captains" of history. It is too bad he missed because he was not in the "In Group."

134

Of Wood, Lieutenant General Willis D. Crittenberger, a corps commander in Italy during World War II, said:

> One of the most valuable characteristics a man in the Army must have is unquestioned leadership. Wood was recognized as a leader. He had it. He far exceeded in his leadership capabilities any man I have ever known.

General Jacob L. Devers, head of the Armored Force, later commander of the Sixth Army Group, considered Wood

> ...a remarkable man—strong and well coordinated physically—keen and alert of mind—and full of deep and sincere emotions. He was equipped to lead men.

General W. M. Hoge, who, as a Major General, assumed command of the 4th Armored Division from the late Major General Hugh J. Gaffey in March of 1945, noted that,

> Wood was much revered and loved by both officers and men of the division.

> I inherited a great division . . . and I attributed many of its fine qualities to the leadership and training fostered by "P" Wood . . . I still marvel at the depth of leadership that was available in all echelons of the division when I took command. I have always felt that "P" Wood was in large measure responsible for this quality.

Lieutnenat General Hobart R. ("Hap") Gay, USA, Retired, the Deputy Chief of Staff and Chief of Staff of the Third Army, characterized Wood as,

> . . . a dynamic leader. He played the game of war with the same drive and vim that he played football. To win . . . .

> I distinctly recall hearing the late General G. S. Patton, Jr., on many occasions, say: "Give me a dozen divisions commanded by leaders like 'P' Wood . . . ."

> General Patton was a long-time friend and a great admirer of Wood. In retrospect I can see they were a great deal alike . . . .

Major General Holmes E. Dager, wartime commander of CC B of the 4th Armored, recalled that Patton described Wood and the division as, "My Sunday punch."

"To the High Command of ETO," Dager wrote, " 'P'

Wood was a top fighting division commander."

To cavalry-man George S. Patton, Wood resembled the famed cavalry leaders, Nathan Forrest and J. E. B. Stuart. Wood, too, "got thar fustest with the mostest." He was aspirin for Patton's headaches and poison to his opponents. About Wood Dager wrote:

> Wood thought big. He saw not only the part 4th Armored had to play, but where and how he could best operate to further the advance of Corps and Third Army. He constantly went over, with Dager, Clarke and others of his Staff, his ideas. He drew maps to illustrate, outlining tactical plans in broad areas suitable for movement of army, corps and divisions. He shaded areas on the map emphasizing terrain most suitable for armored forces, infantry, artillery positions, enveloping tactics and road-nets facilitating movement and supply.

> Held occasionally by conditions natural in war, Wood sweated out these delays, stalking back and forth in or outside his tent, living up to his nickname "Tiger Jack." Inaction irked him to the depth of his soul. He growled: "Here we sit on our tail, watching the Krauts out there on our front build more obstacles and trenches! This delay will cost me too damn many of my people."

> To the end of the war and after, until he died July 2, 1966, "P" Wood was loved, admired and constantly in the mind and heart of his "people," as he always referred to his officers and men.

General O. P. Weyland, then commanding the XIX Tactical Air Command, later to rise to top rank in the Air Force, supported the Third Army's drive across France, and came to know Wood as "a dynamic leader."

> He was aggressive and seized the initiative whenever possible—which was most of the time. He liked to operate independently and moved on many objectives of his own choosing—and he didn't worry too much about losing communications to the rear. In this respect he almost "out-Pattoned" Patton. Whereas more cautious division commanders occasionally warranted some

prodding, "P" just as often had to be restrained . . . .

General "P" Wood epitomized the driving spirit of the 4th Armored Division—to my mind the best in the ETO. He appreciated and fully exploited friendly air cover . . . . I thought he was a great tactician and armored leader . . . .

Lieutenant General Troy H. Middleton, Wood's Corps Commander in the crucial first days of the drive across France, summed it all up when he wrote, in a letter to Wood, 12 April 1962, that "the Lord never produced a better combat leader than John Shirley Wood."

By the evaluations of historians and the verdict of his peers, Wood was a remarkably successful division commander, a leader who honed his division to a fine cutting edge, and who directed it with superb skill to achievements in Europe in World War II that were not excelled, and seldom equalled by any other American division.

However, a recitation of his accomplishments and the evaluations of his peers does not explain the "P" Wood "magic." How did he do it; what secrets of leadership did the man's character and personality hold; what were his methods?

In a passage in his unpublished memoirs, "P" Wood characterized his friend and Army commander, the late General George Patton:

> George Patton was the outstanding warrior of them all in Europe. He understood the nature of combat and the essentials for victory better than any of those placed ahead of him, including Montgomery. He had distinguished himself as a leader of tanks in combat during 1918 and thereafter had applied himself assiduously to the study of warfare and the application of modern weapons in war of movement. He was a believer in the doctrines of indirect approach and deep thrusts into the enemy's vitals, as expressed by Liddell Hart and Fuller between the wars.
>
> More than anyone I have ever known, George Patton was motivated by the desire for personal military glory. His patriotism and religion were real and not assumed,

but to him they served best as a background for the glory of Patton the warrior. He strove to create and maintain the myth of "Old Blood and Guts" by concealing under a hardboiled exterior and roughness of expression his natural fineness of spirit and tenderness of heart that I knew well from personal experience. His mannerism, his pistols, and his panoply of stars were all part of the act. I loved him like a brother . . . .

In this passage, Wood painted, in his description of Patton, a faint image of himself. The two men were, indeed, much alike, personally and professionally. Both were sensitive, complex men; both had warmth of heart and compassion beneath "he-man" exteriors. But Wood was not driven by a thirst for personal glory; rather his motivation was a proprietary pride in the men he commanded. Wood was a commanding figure, but he played command in low key; he did not use the accouterments of command, the trademarks of ivory-handled revolvers, or strapped-on grenades, or the purple passages and roaring expletives of Patton. He was a distinctive figure, but again in low key—polished boots, riding breeches, sunglasses, and visored cap—but his presence needed little sartorial support or professional "props"; it was, naturally, a commanding one.

Unlike Patton, Wood rarely cursed or swore; George Patton's purple passages grated on Wood's ears. He summarized all contempt, dislike, disapproval, and disagreement in one word, *"Stupid!"*—always uttered with an exclamation mark. On at least two occasions Wood adjured Patton to moderate his language—once in Hawaii, when Wood's parents were visiting him; once in England, when Patton spoke to the 4th Armored Division. To Patton, colorful expletives were part of his trademark, his cachet, but it was a measure of the man—and, indicative of the closeness of his relationship with Wood, on both occasions Patton completely complied with Wood's admonitions.

Wood had innate endowments as a leader, endowments which he developed and which the Army helped him to develop in the early part of his 38 years of active duty. He had a commanding presence; he was a big husky man—a natural athlete who excelled at games and played a brisk game of tennis or squash until the day he died at age 78. The rugged frame and the physical constitution to withstand the breaking strain of combat, and the restless, pulsating energy and vitality which could be slaked only by action, gave him the bodily strength and vigor essential to meet the unremitting demands of command in modern war.

Wood's emotional personality belied his gruff exterior. George M. Mardikian has written,

> ... with all that rough and tough appearance, and the demands that he would make, he had a very soft heart for his fellow man and for his troops. All the people I have known had nothing but love and devotion for him.

He was warm-hearted, outgoing, and he had developed fierce but simple loyalties:

Loyalty Up, but rarely personified; rather to the generic Army, which he loved, and to the country which he served with proud devotion. He had difficulty, as many men do, in lending uncritical allegiance to lesser men set above him; especially to men whose mental endowments or moral courage were inferior to his own. But, unlike others like him who held their tongues, Wood was no "yes-man"; he tilted a lance always against the unjust or stupid. This did him no good in a military society, yet when convinced he was right, he said so without mincing words, and to anyone regardless of rank. He was "unorthodox" in a profession that requires, above all, the most conforming orthodoxy. An associate said of him: "He did and said what he believed, whether or not it was the party line."

Loyalty Down. This was Wood's outstanding characteristic as a leader. Any good combat officer must become emotionally involved with his men or he is not a good officer. On the other hand, if he becomes too involved, particularly in heavy combat when casualties are certain to be sizeable, he will either crack or his battlefield judgment will become erratic. Wood *was* involved with his men; he had a burning loyalty to the 4th Armored Division and all who were of it, and a fierce, intense and protective pride in his officers and his men. He cared for his men, and he took care of them.

After the green U.S. forces suffered a humiliating defeat at Kasserine Pass in North Africa in 1943, I recall a remark made to me by General (later Field Marshal) Sir Harold Alexander, the British commander, who was then newly appointed deputy to Eisenhower: "I say you know, your chaps don't wear the old school tie, do they?"

He was referring, in the oblique British way, to the rather sorry performance of some "fresh-caught" U.S. officers—particularly some of lower rank—who had displayed a woeful lack of leadership, and who had committed the cardinal crime of any officer: they had failed to look out for their men. In Britain the public schools had inculcated for centuries a sense of *noblesse oblige* in their graduates; from this class much of the British officer group was drawn, and those who wore the "old school tie" saw that their men ate first, that they slept in as much comfort as conditions permitted, that they were guided, trained, disciplined, cared for, in much the same way—with, of course, military overtones—that a father would care for his son.

West Point, like the British public schools, has always inculcated—in a different way from the British, where class distinctions and the tradition of the squire and the landed gentry have played their part—this sense of duty and obligation downwards. Wood preeminently understood that while Rank Has Its Privileges, it has above all its responsibilities; as a division commander, he rarely invoked the former—he lived as much as possible like his men, frequently in a tent and in the mud; he always accepted and welcomed the latter.

Thus, one of Wood's most conspicuous traits as a military leader was his liking for people, his "compassion," as one of his friends described it, a trait that is rarely associated in the public mind with the stereotype of a general.

Wood himself felt that "the one fundamental quality of true leadership . . . [is] human understanding." In an exchange of letters, in 1961-1962, with Major General Edward B. Sebree, who was undertaking a study of Army leadership for the Human Resources Research Office of

140

George Washington University, Wood wrote that the keys to leading men in battle were,

> . . . warmth, understanding, sympathy, compassion, whatever you want to call it, the intangible essence of human comprehension that emanated from Lee and from Washington.
>
> Jake Devers, Bill Simpson, Joe Stilwell, Sandy Patch, Bolivar Buckner [Lieutenant General Simon Bolivar Buckner, who was killed on Okinawa] to a lesser degree — all had the quality I am talking about, and you can count them on the fingers of one hand . . . .

Patton, he felt,

> . . . was a great warrior — the only higher commander of the Allies who understood the nature and the possibilities of swift victory — but he was not a great leader.

MacArthur's greatness, he felt, was

> . . . of an Olympian sort . . . part of his forces but with a sort of Jovian aloofness, regarding them, except for certain members of his personal and peculiar court, simply as players in the great and tragic drama which he was directing. He established a myth and did not deviate from it . . . .

It was this human understanding, probably more than any other one thing — Wood's interest in them, his dependence on them — that led the men of the 4th Armored to deliver *par excellence* in World War II. They did not want to "let the Old Man down," and they did not. They came to feel, as Wood taught them to feel, that they could do anything, that they were, indeed, in the phraseology of the old cliché, "the best damn division in the best damn corps in the best damn Army in the whole f. . . . Army."

Wood's belief in them made his men believe in themselves and fortified their spirits. In a letter written in 1962 to a division comrade, he wrote that the men of the 4th Armored,

> . . . were a different breed. They were great, and they knew it — like the soldiers of Caesar's Tenth Legion —

141

and I have seen nothing like them in the three wars I was part of in my time.

General Wood's mental capabilities contributed materially to his success as a leader. He had an excellent mind; learning came easily to him, and he retained much of what he learned. He was an easy linguist, and he found no problems with firing tables or, to some, the esoteric gobbledegook of his trade. His mental processes were flexible and quick; sports had taught him to react to unexpected situations, and he was accustomed to making rapid decisions. Wood was the antithesis of indecision; he could understand the tortured gropings of a Hamlet, but he himself, like any man who can lead others, knew always where he wanted to go. His orders were terse, pointed. Before the division embarked for England, Wood, in an address to his troops, said:

This division will attack and attack, and if an order is ever given to fall back, that order will not come from me.

Later, when the division landed in Normandy, Wood is supposed to have issued one order:

Follow me.

Wood later joked that he used one word too many.

He had an *interested* mind, as well as a quick one; in his 40's and 50's he grasped the immense tactical and strategic possibilities of the tank and the aircraft long before younger, and presumably more adaptable men understood them. He had, as Bruce Clarke put it, "a brilliant mind and was a great scholar of military strategy."

Professionally, Wood had no excessive branch-consciousness. His basic arm was artillery, but he had served as an ordnance officer, and he had a general over-view of the combat arms and services, and how each meshed with the other, that was rather rare in the Army of his day. He came to feel, as he grew older, that the linear theories of offense and defense which grew out of the trench stalemate of World War I, and the Infantry School concepts of a "tidied-up" battlefield were too rigid and inflexible. Like Patton and many of the armored officers of their time, he thought the traditional approach was too much one of caution, of static adherence to the "book" solution. Wood was a professional soldier in the best sense; he knew his army and what produced combat results. For some of the trivia of military life he had little use, but he was a "bear" on training, insistent on detail, persistent in the pursuit of perfection.

Lieutenant Colonel David H. Hackworth wrote in the Jan.-Feb. 1967 issue of *Infantry* that,

> ... to win in battle, superbly trained and disciplined soldiers are the vital ingredient, soldiers who have been conditioned by thorough training to react by habit when confronted with the cruel, harsh conditions of battle. The habits learned in training—good or bad—are the same habits the soldier will use in combat. A leader, then, must insure that each of his soldiers is well trained and has developed good habits—habits so deeply ingrained through correct teaching and intensive practice that even under the strain of battle each soldier, automatically, will do the right thing.

Wood's training program was keyed to this end: to the development of sound combat habits, and to flexibility, rapidity and initiative. He tolerated mistakes and corrected them but not the same mistake twice, not repeated mistakes. Performance was required, results expected in the 4th Armored. In his memoirs, Wood himself commented that,

> ... military leadership generally requires a sound basis of military education supplemented by years of study and reflection.
>
> While no particular event or personality or association may be singled out in the formation of an officer's character, the sum total of all such things influences and guides his performance in war.

Wood's methods were simple but effective. When he took over the 4th Armored Division in 1942, he was known, General DeWitt C. Smith recalled,

> ... as old "Paper and Butts," because he insisted so strongly on policing the area that our unit would have an immaculate face.
>
> General Wood had taken over a sloppy division—

sloppy in many senses—and he was determined to strive for perfection in everything.

The General insisted that everyone salute on sight—any distance, senior saluting junior as well as vice versa. He wanted an alert outfit; and a salute was a greeting not a sign of obeisance.

General Wood was forever assembling groups of soldiers around him and telling them . . . they were great . . . they were part of a great outfit . . . they and it were going to be better yet . . . all for one, and one for all . . . and that the Division would never move backward. We believed him.

General Abrams recalled that in the heat of the Desert Training Center Wood required sleeves of fatigues to be rolled down, collars buttoned.

These were not measures calculated to make a commander popular. General Bruce Clarke, then Chief of Staff of the division, spoke to Wood about these requirements:

> Wood was a strong character and a strong leader . . . . He had firm ideas about things that he liked and disliked and placed requirements on his officers and men in the fields of wearing of equipment and uniforms, tactical disposition during field training, the care and handling of vehicles, and other things, many of which were unpopular. At one time in an evening discussion period, I pointed out these requirements to him and asked him if he felt the effort that he put into them was not excessive for the practical results which he achieved. His answer gave me an insight into the problems of training and preparing troops for emergencies in battle which I have never forgotten.
>
> He stated that in case of an emergency or in battle, a commander was required to place upon his officers and men many requirements that were unpopular and for which time was not available for hesitation. The thought of being popular or unpopular should never enter the mind of a commander. He pointed out that a commander who was unable to obtain compliance with unpopular

requirements from his officers and men during training and during preparation for combat, would not be able to obtain prompt compliance with his requirements to meet emergencies or to attack an enemy in battle. He said that the requirements he placed in the training period served three purposes: they conditioned his command to carry out promptly his instructions; the way which his men carried out these requirements served as a constant measure to him of his hold on his officers and men; and, they—with other things—helped to instill a fierce pride in the division.

Wood gave his commanders much initiative and encouraged innovation in training and in the development of tactics. It was thus not by accident that the 4th Armored produced more stars—more leaders destined for general's rank—than nearly any other division in Europe.

Wood tried everything in the book—and much that was not; ideas were grist to his mill, and tactical dispositions, tank fire while moving, artillery concentrations, mine-clearing, all-around defense, map reading, reconnaissance, armored infantry tactics, and night operations were practiced again and again until the units were letter-perfect. Each officer came to know the others' voice over the telephone or radio; call signs and code names were unnecessary.

During the training, the division's units were thoroughly "scrambled"; there was no rigid assignment of units to specific combat commands. Each unit was trained to work in harmony with every other unit. Battalions were "traded off one for another, added to or taken away from combat commands in the middle of training exercises till we learned to make these switches with no dimunition of effectiveness," General Hal Pattison recalled.

There gradually grew up the intimacy of close association, of common striving for a common purpose, and of friendship which, when blended, makes for teamwork. General Jacob L. Devers described "P" Wood's methods as "simple":

> He issued his orders orally and left his staff to write them up in proper form and simple language so that each

element knew just what it had to do. He then went where the going was roughest, and provided the effective leadership because he took full advantage of the time element. Supply was automatic. His intelligence was always short and to the point. His men knew him intimately and would follow him anywhere . . . .

But always, he looked out for his men with an almost jealous pride. General Smith recalled:

> When he captured the Wehrmacht's stores of French wines and liquors, an issue was made to the Division. The priority of issue began with the rifle squads and tank crews and moved upward after that.
>
> Precisely the same was true when we first received steak and white bread after many weeks of K-Rations.

Wood himself on many occasions ruminated about his methods and the art of military leadership. In a letter during the war to Liddell Hart, the British military critic and one of many friends and admirers of General Wood from many walks of life throughout the world, Wood described his "principles, all of them old for thousands of years":

1. De l'audace.
2. Indirect approach.
3. Direct oral orders—no details, only missions.
4. Movement in depth always—allows flexibility and security of flanks.
5. Disregard of old ideas of flank security, i.e., by other units on left and right.
6. Organization of supply (taking rations, gas, and ammunition in rolling reserves).
7. Personal communication with commanders (only possible by plane now).
8. Never taking counsel of fears.
9. Never fearing what "They" will say or do ("They being the same old bogie—high officialdom or general opinion).
10. Trusting people in rear to do their part (a trust sometimes misplaced, but not generally).

At the 18th convention of the 4th Armored Division Association Wood said in an address:

> The main purpose of our military establishment should be to produce leaders of American fighting men in war, not to develop egg-heads .... the fundamental qualification for a leader of fighting men is understanding of the human heart and spirit—and this cannot be evaluated by polygraphs or computers .... I am sure that war, as always, will require more of the Farragut type— "Damn the torpedoes, Full Speed Ahead!" than the egg-head variety—"Man the Computers, Proceed with the Count-Down!"

In 1960, six years before his death, General Wood was asked by General Smith, then a major, to expound his principles of leadership. His answer reveals the man, his methods and his triumphs:

> I wish I were able to draw up a set of rules for developing a fighting unit like the 4th Armored Division. I am convinced that, as you say, it was great, and that it was almost unique in its fighting characteristics and *esprit,* but it did not conform to rules. In fact, that is perhaps its most outstanding characteristic. Outsiders could never understand what made us so different nor just how we operated.
>
> Of course, there are certain principles of command, which, like the well-known principles of war, have been set down in the texts and regulations and have been learned and repeated by rote in our schools. Last year, General [Bruce C.] Clarke, who is a great fellow for analysis, sent me an admirable document outlining do's and don'ts for unit commanders. All this sort of thing certainly furnishes a thoughtful commander, with a desire to learn, a good basis for his study and reflection, but for the production of a fighting organization like the 4th Armored Division it would be like giving an artist a set of draughtman's rules and a color chart and asking him to produce the Mona Lisa. There is very little science in command—it is merely the most difficult of arts, done

with the lightest of touches!

There is tradition and pride and loyalty in a fighting team. We have paid far too little attention to conserving tradition in our Army—the Marines have done better—but if it has not been conserved, it must be created. A commander must have a fierce and personal pride in his command, and it must extend to every man and every unit of the outfit. The chief expects no loyalty that he does not engender, for loyalty begins only at the top and it grows and redoubles as it moves out and down and back again. There is no doubt about these things in the mind of a commander—they are part of him.

All for one and one for all! is the only slogan for a fighting organization. Every man in it must feel that he is individually responsible for its reputation and its actions and that he will be backed by his commanders and comrades in any act of individual initiative.

Many commanding officers make the mistake of fostering and encouraging competition among their units and even among the individuals of their command. There is nothing worse! The only goal must be perfection—perfection in attaining the standards set by the commander, perfection in team play, perfection in concerted and combined action—and every man must be convinced that he is personally responsible for it.

This may all seem like a set of high ideals and fine sounding words; but it can't be written off that way, for the 4th Armored Division stands as an example of the application of the principles I have tried to outline.

If a commander is granted the time for arriving at some degree of the perfection he seeks for his organization, he can count himself as supremely lucky—and I had that luck with our 4th Armored Division. Once achieved, even in part, the morale and *esprit* engendered live on—a growing thing, motivating and inspiring even the newest of recruits and replacements.

*   *   *   *   *   *   *   *

What strategic and tactical role did Wood and the 4th

Armored Division play in the history of World War II?

In a war of armies and army groups, a war of the scope and immensity of the second great war, division commanders usually have only tangential influence upon strategy. They and their divisions can and do affect the big picture, but the broad plans, the "How-To-Win," are made by other men— men sometimes far remote in time and space from the blood and sweat of the battlefield.

Wood and his division nevertheless found themselves, in the summer of 1944, at the vortex of the U.S. strategic plans; the decisions Wood made and helped to make, and the things the division did, influenced the course of the war in France.

The 4th Armored Division spearheaded the breakout of the Third Army from Normandy and rampaged into the Brittany peninsula in late July and early August of 1944. Pre-invasion planning had envisaged the capture of the Brittany ports as essential to the augmentation and expansion of the Allied supply line in France. But the entire scenario of conquest was thrown out of kilter by the determined German resistance in the hedgerow country of Normandy and then by the enemy rout and collapse following the break-out.

It had always been thought that the decisive battle of the French campaign would be fought to the eastwards, in the interior of France, and that there would be a long pause on the Seine for regrouping and resupply, but the entire tactical and strategic situation in France was in a state of flux, with the enemy completely disorganized following the breakout.

Wood was probably one of the first to see this and to appreciate its implications. His division cut the base of the Brittany peninsula, as ordered, and probed the defenses of Lorient, but, as early as 2 August, Wood had commenced to dispose part of his division towards the east, ready to roar towards Paris and the Swiss frontier. To him, attacks upon the fortified ports were a waste of time and power. Wood had his way—belatedly. By mid-August the responsibility of containing Lorient was turned over to another division, and Wood drove to the east in his famous sweep across France.

Martin Blumenson comments in the official U.S. History,

Breakout and Pursuit, that "despite . . . impressive achievement, the 4th Armored . . . had not taken the port city assigned [Lorient]." He added that, "A serious effort launched immediately after the arrival of the division might still have taken the fortress." Wood himself scouted this, and Blumenson added:

> In mid-August, as the Germans in western Europe seemed to be in the process of complete disintegration, the failure to take Lorient and Quiberon seemed less important than it would have seemed in July. By late September, Lorient and Quiberon were quite forgotten.

Some critics, notably those most concerned with the responsiblity of supply, have maintained that the 4th Armored Division's failure to capture Lorient and the Third Army's failure to capture the rest of the Brittany ports initiated the supply difficulties that were later to hamper and slow up or halt the Allied armies as they approached the German frontier. It is true that the early possession of these ports and their rapid development would have materially increased the flow of supplies into France before the Westwall was reached, and it is true that the original Overlord plan envisaged their early capture.

But the plan was unrealistic in two respects: it not only failed to envisage the rapid retreat of the Germans and the consequent remoteness of Brittany from the fighting front, but it implied seizure of undamaged harbors, lock gates, and docks. In any event, the ports of Brittany, destroyed during the assaults upon them, were logistically useless and geographically irrelevant.

Wood's swift recognition of the changed situation after the breakout and his instinctive positioning of his division to drive to the East, rather than to get bogged down in street fighting against fortified citadels, was the correct one; both General George S. Patton and Lieutenant General Troy Middleton, Wood's corps commander, subsequently said so.

In a letter to Wood dated 12 April 1962, General Middleton, who was then President Emeritus of Louisiana

State University, said flatly:

I do know this, and it is: Ike [Eisenhower] and Brad [General Bradley] could have left a Corporals guard at Rennes, and followed you to Paris, Belgium, etc. and the Battle of the Bulge [the last German offensive in Belgium in December 1944] would never have happened. I presume, however, they felt it was imperative to secure Brest as a port.

In *The Liberation of France,* written in 1965, B. H. Liddell Hart, the British military critic, pointed out:

When the breakout came at Avranches, on July 31, only a few scattered German battalions lay in the ninety-mile-wide corridor between that point and the Loire. So American spearheads could have driven eastward unopposed. But the Allied High Command threw away the best chance of exploiting this great opportunity by sticking to the outdated pre-invasion programme, in which a westward move to capture the Brittany ports was to be the next step.

The breakout at Avranches was made by the U.S. 4th Armored Division under John S. Wood. I had spent two days with him shortly before the invasion and he had impressed me as being more conscious of the possibilities of a deep exploitation and the importance of speed than anyone else. Even Patton had then, in discussion with me, echoed the prevailing view at the top that the Allied forces must "go back to 1918 methods" and could not repeat the kind of deep and swift armoured drives that the Germans, especially Guderian and Rommel, had carried out in 1940.

Telling me later what happened after the breakout, Wood said:

"There was no conception of far-reaching directions for armour in the minds of our top people, nor of supplying such thrusts. When the Army Command did react, its orders consisted of sending its two flank armoured divisions back, 180 degrees away from the main enemy, to engage in siege operations against Lorient and Brest.

151

Maj. Gen. Wood in his M-8 Armored car, Avranches, July 1944.

August 4th was that black day. I protested long, loud and violently—and pushed my tank columns into Chateaubriant [without orders] and my armoured cavalry to the out-skirts of Angers and along the Loire, ready to advance [east on Chartres]. I could have been there, in the enemy vitals, in two days. But no! We were forced to adhere to the original plan—with the only armour available, and ready to cut the enemy to pieces. It was one of the colossally stupid decisions of the war."

The diversion to capture the Brittany ports brought no benefit. For the Germans in Brest held out until September 19—forty-four days after Patton had pre-maturely announced its capture—while Lorient and St. Nazaire remained in the enemy's hands until the end of the war.

In retrospect, it is certain that the Brittany ports could not have been captured in time enough or undamaged enough

152

to have served any useful purpose.

Moreover, the supply shortages that began to be evident were not caused primarily by the lack of these ports but by "the deficiency of transportation facilities," as the Army's official history puts it. Huge tonnages had been brought in over the invasion beaches and through Cherbourg and the Normandy ports. A more streamlined and more efficient supply organization might have produced even more startling statistics; there was much grumbling in the Third Army and among other tactical units about the service of supply—some of it justified.

The wasteful habits of the Allies, and, particularly, the "broad front" strategy, which put the maximum strain upon the service of supply without allocating sufficient supplies to any one Army to permit continuous mobility, plus fanatical German resistance, were responsible for the check of the Allies near the German frontier.

General Wood maintained until the end of his life that if the Third Army had not been halted by a lack of gas the war could have been won much sooner. General Patton and many of those who served with him believed the momentum of the Third Army's thrust could have been carried into the vitals of Germany in the fall of 1944.

A study, conducted by the U.S. Army Armored School in 1948-49, entitled "Armor in the Exploitation—or the 4th Armored Division Across France," summed up, in its conclusions, the general belief of many tankers that the war might have been won in 1944:

> The 4th Armored Division halted on the Moselle River line and remained immobile for a period of ten days. The Support Services were unable to supply the 4th Armored (and other elements of the Third Army) over the overextended supply lines at a time when the Division was unimpeded by the enemy. But for the time being, at least, the great opportunity was lost. When they were again able to go forward, with gas tanks full and ammunition racks replenished, the Nazi had reformed his lines. Many months of bitter fighting were to pass before real progress was to be made.

No stronger lesson on the importance of logistics to tactical operations could be related. Here was an armored division, one that had already made history, on the threshhold of what may well have been the prelude to final victory in the west. The enemy was reeling; his forces disrupted and disorganized. He was no longer capable of maintaining a continuous battle line nor did he possess sufficient mobility to stay the mighty thrusts of our armor. It is now only a matter for conjecture how long and how far the 4th Armored Division could have continued eastward had their logistical support been adequate to the occasion. This is in no way a criticism of our supply forces in France. They performed magnificently, supplying the ever-growing numbers of American units on the continent. Sufficient transport was not available to keep extending supply lines in order that combat units would not have to halt for logistical reasons. Nevertheless, the enforced ten day delay enabled the harried Germans to reform a semblance of a line and to man their Siegfried Line defenses.

In their belief in the "single thrust" into Germany rather than the broad front—or attack all along the line strategy—Patton's supporters found themselves curiously at one with the adherents of a general few of them admired, Field Marshal Montgomery. Both Patton and Montgomery criticized the broad front approach, a strategy approved by the Combined Chiefs of Staff and by General Eisenhower; both Patton and "Monty" wanted priority in resources and virtually a free hand to ramble and to roll.

Liddell Hart supports the thesis that the war could easily have been ended in September 1944:

> The best chance of a quick finish was probably lost when the "gas" was turned off from Patton's tanks in the last week of August, when they were 100 miles nearer to the Rhine, and its bridges, than the British.
>
> Patton had a keener sense than anyone else on the Allied side of the key importance of persistent pace in pursuit. He was ready to exploit in any direction—indeed, on August 23rd he had proposed that his army

should drive north instead of east. There was much point in his subsequent comment: "one does not plan and then try to make circumstances fit those plans. One tries to make plans fit the circumstances. I think the difference between success and failure in high command depends upon its ability, or lack of it, to do just that."

But the root of all the Allied troubles at this time of supreme opportunity was that none of the top planners had foreseen such a complete collapse of the enemy as occurred in August. They were not prepared, mentally or materially, to exploit it by a rapid long-range thrust.

Wood saw the opportunity and, to the best of his ability, capitalized on it. If the Third Army had been given its head, if the 4th Armored had been turned eastward in Brittany a week to ten days sooner, if . . . if . . . if . . . .

Certainly it is true, as Liddell Hart noted, that "persistent pace and pressure is the key to success in any deep penetration or pursuit, and even a day's pause may forfeit it."

The Germans were given their breathing spells, in August, in Brittany, and again in September, as the Allied armies were closing up to the German frontier, and they took advantage of it. They rallied miraculously, fought ferociously, and the war went on through many more months of agony.

No one can evaluate with certainty these might-have-beens of history—the question raised by the belated change in plans in Brittany, the supply difficulties, the broad-front versus the single-thrust strategy; no one can say with assurance that even if the retreating Germans had been pursued relentlessly without halt or pause that the war would have ended in 1944. This writer is inclined to doubt it. There was still too much fight left in the Germans, and a totalitarian dictatorship which has everything to lose by defeat can always muster last-gasp efforts, no matter what irrational purpose they may serve.

But it is clear that Wood's strategic appreciation was sound—in Brittany in August, again in Northern France in September. He wanted to take time by the forelock, to exploit opportunity, to maintain mobility.

Tactically, even more than strategically, Wood left a

major mark upon the history of World War II. He was a master of armored tactics; the 4th Armored exemplified fire power, mobility, mass times momentum. Wood described his methods in his memoirs:

> Contrary to the practice in many other armored divisions, we had no separation into fixed or rigid combat commands. To me the division was a reservoir of force to be applied in different combinations as circumstances indicated, and which could be changed as needed in the course of combat by a commander in close contact with the situation at the front. There is no time or place for detailed orders, limiting lines or zones, phase lines, limited objectives, or other restraints . . . . It must drive fast and hard in given directions in columns of all arms with the necessary supply, maintenance, and supporting elements present in each column, ready for action to the front or toward the flanks. As long as we were in depth we were not disturbed about our flanks, since we could counter any threat of action by the rearward elements. Each column was self-sustaining for prolonged action, and only the vital essential of fuel could limit or halt our action. In war of movement the supply of ammunition is not a major problem and the matter of food was taken care of by loading each vehicle with enough packaged rations for ten days or more of continous operation. The small packaged ration with men trained to conserve it and subsist on it for long periods was one of the great aids for mobile operations by our armored units.
>
> I commanded my division by keeping contact with my column commanders from jeep or Cub plane. My staff was occupied mainly in keeping contact with me and seeing that my directions for supply and maintenance were carried out. They also tried to get word back to higher commanders, but in the extremely fluid operations after the breakout it was up to higher headquarters to find us, and we hoped now and then that they would not be able to do it.

These seemingly "informal" tactics and this *ad hoc* system of command were far more "organized" than they

France, 1944. Maj. Gen. Wood, CG, 4th Armored Division, confers with his commander, Col. Bruce Clarke. Seated in rear of "peep" is 1st Lt. Wetherall, Aide de Camp.

appeared; they had been rehearsed so often in training that the division worked like a drill team, and each man performed his role in the ballet of battle—seemingly spontaneously, actually because his actions and reactions had become almost a part of his subconscious.

Brigadier General Hal C. Pattison, who in 1944 was executive officer of Combat Command A of the 4th Armored Division, described some of the division's methods in a paper, "Typical Armored Combat Command Operations," prepared for the Command and General Staff College at Fort Leavenworth:

> . . . supplies carried on every truck exceeded by at least 50 per cent the rated capacity of the vehicle. Seven days' rations on every vehicle for its crew became SOP . . . .
>
> Columns were always made up of the combined arms . . . with a series of tank-infantry teams married up

in the column. A squad of engineers was always with the leading team, the rest of a platoon with the leading part of the main body. This platoon always had two truck-loads of bridging equipment with it . . . .

Artillery was always well forward in the column . . . .

No vehicle was allowed to halt on the road if there was a way off. If the head of the column stopped, the units behind kept moving to a point where they could get off the road into an assembly area of some kind and put out local security. This became known as "coiling" . . . everything possible was done to keep up the speed of the advance for one of the first lessons learned was that much of the security of the column derived from the speed of its advance . . . .

. . . medical and maintenance companies [were] attached to the combat command and [went] every-where with it . . . . The service companies of the attached units, the medical and maintenance companies made up the combat command trains and they marched at the tail of the combat column . . . .

. . . the flexibility of the organization of the armored division was repeatedly proven by the ability of the command to change task force organizations in the middle of an operation and by the frequent change of organization of the combat command itself . . . .

. . . the technique of attacking cities [by the 4th Armored Division] . . . was the same technique that the Russians used in employing the equivalent of 20 American armored divisions in the capture of Berlin . . . this technique is to attack on a very narrow front with a balanced force of tanks, infantry and engineers supported with adequate artillery . . . avoiding entering the perimeter of the city on streets . . . instead attacking through yards, alleyways and other such areas on a front of 400 to 500 yards . . . . The assaulting force penetrates in this manner to a depth of two or three blocks, then returns to the streets as their axis of advance. Side streets are blocked and a narrow zone cleared . . . consolidation of a central

158

area is effected, and attacks then made simultaneously in all directions . . . .

A study, made after the war by the Armored School of the 4th Armored's operations, stressed: mission type orders; no phase lines; keep going until stopped by the enemy; use of secondary roads; close integration of combined arms; boldness in execution; flexibility.

What pertinence do such armored tactics have for today or tomorrow? Are they "old hat" in modern armies, interesting historically but valueless in application to contemporary wars?

Wood did not think so. In 1950 he addressed the French Ecole de Guerre, from which he had graduated so many years earlier, on the employment of tanks and armored divisions. He drew heavily on his experiences in World War II but also addressed himself to the future. The tank, he still felt, was,

> . . . the most powerful and maneuverable tool that we have at our disposition today for ground warfare.

> It is possible that the tank of the future, powered by atomic energy, will be able to fly, swim and roll over all types of terrain . . . . It should not be too heavy, but capable of rapid maneuver.

It should be air transportable, he thought, and possibly armed with smooth bore cannon, firing finned projectiles— a prescient blueprint of the weapons in service today.

General Wood was tacitly critical of the rigidity and the size of the armored division as it evolved in the post-war years; it should never have been based "on fixed or rigid military thought." The large-scale employment of tanks "demands control of the air, either complete or at least locally . . . the closest liaison between aviation and tanks . . . there should be no mutually exclusive combat in warfare." Later, in his memoirs, Wood recorded another prescient passage about the utility of tanks in today's conflicts.

> Both Russia and the West have become aware that any nuclear conflict would destroy the objectives for

which war is waged and both are seeking other means of achieving their ends. For the Russians "peaceful co-existence" offers a profitable atmosphere for their unchanging policy of economic pressure and subversive action against capitalism in all lands, while the Western strategists still toy with the idea of limited war to contain Communism, even of limited nuclear war with "escalation thresholds" to aviod all-out nuclear conflict. The Russians are far more logical in their insistence that there can be no such thing as a limited nuclear war and that the employment of nuclear weapons tactically will inevitably lead to the employment of others strategically. Neither side desires a nuclear holocaust but both base their preparations for war on the assumption that any future conflict between them will begin by missile attacks with nuclear weapons. Thus the nuclear armament race continues unabated.

There is, however, no diminution in the preparation of conventional forces. More and more emphasis is placed on the development of airborne forces of all arms, and the tank is recognized as the weapon best suited for ground operations in a nuclear conflict. With the possibility of increased speed and maneuverability over all terrains due to the development of lighter materials for armor and lighter armament such as guided missiles coupled with the possibility of radiation absorption and interior pressure systems to protect the crews in areas infected by nuclear explosions armored forces will certainly be those most capable of exploiting the effects of initial missile bombardments. Utilized in accordance with the principles of flexibility in constituting and changing the composition of units, immediate and close control by commanders on the spot, rapid dispersion and equally rapid concentrations of self-sustaining columns for action in depth—all with constant air support—the same principles developed and perfected by the 4th Armored Division in battle—armored forces of the future moving in decisive directions will administer the coup de grace to a shaken enemy.

The Russians are developing their armored forces for use in this manner, as clearly and succinctly stated by thier Marshal Rominstrov in a recent issue of Izvestia: "Their high degree of resistance to nuclear attacks, their maneuverability, and their striking force, will permit armored elements to penetrate rapidly in the zones subjected to atomic bombardment and to complete the work begun by the missiles. For these reasons, the tanks are not outmoded and indeed constitute the best weapon of the ground forces. By attacking day and night they will drive deep into enemy territory and clear the way for the rest of the ground forces. If necessary they can operate independently in the rear areas of an enemy, without the support of infantry elements, which may be dropped by air into their zone of action. We may conclude that the modern tank in following along the directions opened up by missile attacks can attain the desired objectives with minimum delay . . . ."

On a nuclear battlefield and even in large-scale conventional combat the tank still retains some, but by no means all, of the combat effectiveness it developed so highly in World War II. In mountainous Korea and in the rice paddies, swamps, plateaus and jungles of Vietnam it has blasted a role for itself with its fire power and mobility.

Yet General Wood, had he lived through the early years of the 1970's, might well have modified the views he expressed more than a decade earlier. He was no static thinker, immovably wed to the past, and he would undoubtedly have seen that the age of precision weapons, the age of highly-accurate guided missiles capable of homing on their targets, would greatly increase the tank's vulnerability and limit its tactical capabilities. The last days of U.S. participation in the Vietnam war, and the immense tank casualties of the "Yom Kippur" war in the Middle East dramatized the radically changed battlefield of today.

More important, the tactical principles developed by the 4th Armored Division—quick "tail-gate" decisions, oral orders, constant momentum, continuous aerial cover, mobility and flexibility and audacity—have universal application to

161

the art of war. The same principles, and many of the same methods, that proved so successful in the 4th Armored Division's sweep across France were the hallmark—with modifications—of the 1st Cavalry Division Airmobile, with helicopters substituted for tanks. Thus, the principles Wood taught still have enduring validity in the Army of today and tomorrow.

But weapons change and, with them, tactics. More important by far, and valid for all time until man loses the aggressive instinct, is the conviction that Wood so often expressed: that men are the arbiters of battle.

As John Albright wrote in the Jan.-Feb., 1972, issue of *Armor* magazine,

> John Shirley Wood gave modern armor much of its unique quality, so much so that it seems that the essential spirit of Armor of today began with the highly professional career soldier who took command of a mixed group of inductees, old Army noncoms, reservists and a few regular officers and blended men and machines into one of the finest organizations in the long and proud history of American arms.

Wood created a tradition and dramatized an eternal truth: that men, not machines, make war.

Wood's leadership, indeed, his entire Army career, emphasized the role of man in battle. To him his soldiers were human beings, not mere "bodies," and he remained convinced until his death that man was the key to victory. His thoughts about the role of man, recorded in his memoirs, were profound and they have been stressed often in the past. Yet, as he saw, they need eternal repetition in this mechanistic age:

> The creation of effective fighting forces is a vital thing for the defense of our country. Under present conditions and conceptions of future war there will not be time for the mobilization and training of large forces such as was possible in former wars. Sufficient force must be available from the start to prevent disaster, and they must be kept in a state of combat readiness. This requires

constant leadership of the highest quality. It cannot be obtained from any ingenious assortments of computers, push-buttons, and machines, although they will all be used. The men who man them are, as always, the ultimate weapon.

Wood's whole philosophy was really the triumph of man. Above all, he agreed with John Stuart Mill, who, more than a century ago, characterized war far better than the most vocal beatniks have ever done:

> War is an ugly thing, but not the ugliest thing: the decayed and degraded state of moral and patriotic feeling which thinks nothing worth war is worse. A man who has nothing which he cares about more than his personal safety is a miserable creature who has no chance of being free, unless made and kept so by the exertions of better men than himself.

EPILOGUE

GENERAL JOHN SHIRLEY WOOD, USMA, CLASS OF 1912, was born in Monticello, Arkansas, on 11 January 1888. He died in Reno, Nevada, on 2 July 1966 and was buried in the West Point cemetery in the setting he so greatly loved.

When he returned to the United States from France in December 1944, General Wood was assigned, after a rest, as Commanding General, Armored Replacement Center, Fort Knox, Kentucky. He retired after the war in 1946 and joined the Intergovernmental Committee for Refugees as Director of Field Operations in Germany and Austria. Subsequently, when this organization became part of the International Refugees Organization in 1947, General Wood became chief of mission in Austria, with headquarters in Salzburg and Vienna from 1947 to the end of 1951. His stay in Austria was enhanced by warm friendships, particularly when it became known that the General had been instrumental in restoring the famous Lipizzaner stables, which had been moved by the Germans from Austria to France, to their rightful owners in Vienna. General Wood joined the United Nations Korean Reconstruction Agency when IRO had finished its task in Europe, and served as chief of mission in

Tokyo and Korea, and later, until the end of 1953, he was its representative with the United Nations in Geneva.

General Wood settled in Reno, Nevada, and was civil defense director there from 1957 to 1959. He remained keenly interested in the problems of the nation and of the world, and continued his correspondence and contacts with friends from many countries until his death. He read many U.S. and foreign papers and journals and his mind, like his body, was restless and active until the last.

In his own "autobituary," General Wood wrote of himself:

> He loved life, its comedy and its laughter . . . . He liked people generally, but he was not gregarious and he detested crowds. He loved beauty and grace and harmonious rhythm (he was a great rose fancier), in every form and hated nothing except meanness and cruelty. His friendships and loyalties were deep and abiding and he could not understand nor condone disloyalty.

The genesis of General Wood's nickname "Tiger Jack" is given by "Wes" Gallagher, then as Associated Press war correspondent and, in 1974, General Manager of the AP, in an article in *Liberty Magazine,* reprinted in "What They Said About the Fourth Armored Division." Gallagher states,

> . . . that the cognomen "Tiger Jack" was conferred on Wood by one of the 4th Armored Division's cub observation pilots . . . [Wood], a long-time crony of the rough, tough, Third Army's pistol-packing commander . . . [was one of the] few subordinate generals . . . not intimidated by Patton's roars of disapproval . . . When Patton roars, Wood roars right back at him. The pacing [a restless habit of General Wood's] and roaring prompted . . . [the nickname] "Tiger Jack."

A Fort Knox study at the Armored School, "Armor in the Exploitation (The 4th Armored Division Across France to the Moselle River)," 1948-1949, comments:

Fort Knox, KY. Maj. Gen. Wood, CG, Armored Replacement Center with Gen. "Vinegar Joe" Stilwell and Brig. Gen. Robinette.

Salzburg, Austria 1950. Maj. Gen. Wood, USA Retired, as Chief of Mission in Austria of the International Refugees Organization, confers with his good friend and West Point classmate, Lt. Gen. Geoffrey Keyes, C.G., U.S. Forces, Austria.

Major General John S. Wood, Retired, Wartime Commanding General of the 4th Armored Division addresses officers and men of the Division at Goppingen, Germany. Left to right: Gen. Wood; Lt. Gen. Waters, V Corps CG; Maj. Gen. Polk, 4th Armored Division Commanding General; Brig. Gen. Grahm, Assistant Division Commander.

Army War College, Carlisle Barracks, PA. 1965. Maj. Gen. Wood with left to right: Gen. Creighton W. Abrams, then Army Vice Chief of Staff; Col. John S. Wood, Jr.; Maj. Gen. Eugene A. Salet, Commandant, U.S. Army War College.

This great advance, spearheaded by armor, bore out the importance and the necessity of using tank units in modern war. By Sept. 15, 1944, few people questioned the important role of armor in the successful waging of land warfare. The faith and perseverance of two great American soldiers, Major General Adna R. Chaffee and General George S. Patton, Jr., came to fruition on the battlefields of France. The contribution of these two men in winning World War II can never be exaggerated. Since 1919, and in the face of severe criticism and skepticism they never lost faith in the tank as a mighty and decisive weapon of war, nor did they waver in their role of foremost exponents of armored employment "en masse."

The 4th Armored and "P" Wood were the proudest exemplars of Mobile Warfare.

APPENDICES
★ ★

APPENDIX I

ORGANIC UNITS OF THE FOURTH ARMORED DIVISION

8th TANK BATTALION

35th TANK BATTALION

37th TANK BATTALION

10th ARMORED INFANTRY BATTALION

51st ARMORED INFANTRY BATTALION

53rd ARMORED INFANTRY BATTALION

24th ARMORED ENGINEER BATTALION

22nd ARMORED FIELD ARTILLERY BATTALION

66th ARMORED FIELD ARTILLERY BATTALION

94th ARMORED FIELD ARTILLERY BATTALION

25th CAVALRY RECONNAISSANCE SQUADRON, MECHANIZED

126th ARMORED ORDNANCE MAINTENANCE BATTALION

46th ARMORED MEDICAL BATTALION

HEADQUARTERS AND HEADQUARTERS BATTERY, DIVISION ARTILLERY

CC A HEADQUARTERS AND HEADQUARTERS COMPANY

CC B HEADQUARTERS AND HEADQUARTERS COMPANY

RESERVE COMMAND

DIVISION HEADQUARTERS COMPANY

144th ARMORED SIGNAL COMPANY

TRAINS HEADQUARTERS AND HEADQUARTERS COMPANY

FORWARD ECHELON, 4th ARMORED DIVISION HEADQUARTERS

REAR ECHELON, 4th ARMORED DIVISION HEADQUARTERS

4th ARMORED DIVISION MILITARY POLICE PLATOON

4th ARMORED DIVISION BAND

8th TANK BATTALION

In September 1943, the 4th Armored Division was reorganized into a "light" Armored Division . . . the 8th Tank Bn. came into being joining the 35th and 37th Tank Battalions. It was fondly christened "The Rolling Eight Ball" by Lt. Col. Edgar T. Conley, the commanding officer. Organized 9/10/43 from 3rd Bn. of the 35th Armd. Rgt.

CAMPAIGNS: Normandy, Northern France, Ardennes-Alsace, Rhineland, Central Europe.

DECORATIONS: Distinguished Unit Citation: "ARDENNES," 22 Dec. 1944, 27 March 1945. WD GO 54-45.
French Fourragere: "NORMANDY" and "MOSELLE RIVER" 27 July, 11 Aug. '44 and 12-29 Sep '44 DA GO 43-50.

MOTTO: "Unity . . . Honor . . . Courage."

DESCRIPTION: The insignia was chosen by a War Bond contest held among the members of the 8th Tank Battalion in July 1945. It was designed and submitted by Tech. 4th Grade Raymond C. Smith, then draftsman, assigned to Battalion Hdqrts. Smith was awarded a twenty-five (25) dollar War Bond.

The insignia is framed by a green wreath in the shape of an inverted horseshoe, upon which are superimposed five battle stars denoting the campaigns in Europe...in which the 8th Tank Bn., participated. A golden ribbon along the top and bottom of the wreath has the battalion motto "Honor, Courage, Unity" printed upon it in black letters. The blue background of the insignia is divided by a streak of lightning signifying striking power. A large, black figure "8" outlined in gold occupies the upper half of the background while a medium tank in gold is placed in the lower half.

COMMANDERS IN COMBAT: Lt. Col. Edgar T. Conley, Jr., Lt. Col. Henry P. Heid, Jr., Major Thomas G. Churchill, Lt. Col. Albin F. Irzyk.

COMMANDER IN OCCUPATION: Major Thornton B. McGlamery.

The 8th Tank became the 11th Constabulary Sqdn. in Memmingen, Germany and today, the 8th Tank Bn. has been redesignated as the 508th Tank Battalion.

35th TANK BATTALION

When the 4th Armored Division was activated in April 15, 1941, the 5th Armored Regiment had already been activated in Jan. 13th, 1941 and assigned to the new 4th Armored Division on the Division's activation day. On May 8th, 1941 it was redesignated as the 35th Armored Regiment. In September 1943 the division was reorganized into a "light" armored division and the 35th Armored Regiment became the 35th Tank Bn. . . . less the 1st and 3rd battalions, Band, Maintenance, Service and Recon Bns. The 3rd battalion becoming the 8th Tank Bn., and Recon Bn., became Troop D, 25th Cavalry Sqdrn. 1st Bn. became the 771st Tank Bn. and was relieved from assignment to the 4th A.D. (it supported the 84th and 102nd Divs.: NETO).

CAMPAIGNS: Normandy, Northern France, Ardennes-Alsace, Rhineland, Central Europe.

DECORATIONS: Distinguished Unit Citation: "ARDENNES," 22 Dec. 1944, 27 March 1945. WD GO 54-45.
French Fourragere: "NORMANDY" and "MOSELLE RIVER" 27 July, 11 Aug. '44 and 12-29 Sept. '44 DA GO 43-50.
French Croix de Guerre w/Palm for Normandy and Moselle River.

MOTTO: "Vincere vel mori." (To conquer or die)

DESCRIPTION: The coat of arms originally approved for the 35th Armored Regiment on May 30, 1942. The shield is green, the color of the Armored Force during World War II. The armadillo being characterized by the qualities of invulnerability, ferociousness, protection and endurance, alludes to the elements which are vital if the 35th is to pursue successfully its duties. The fluer-de-lis represents service in France during W.W. II and the palm branch is indicative of victory achieved at the end of the war. The original crest did not have the fleur-de-lis on top until after victory in Europe.

COMMANDERS IN COMBAT: Lt. Col. Bill A. Bailey, Lt. Col. Delk M. Oden.

COMMANDERS IN OCCUPATION: Major Hambleton B. Carpenter.

The 35th Tank Bn. was assigned to the 4th Armored Division on 25 Feb. 1953 and reactivated 15 June 1954 at Ft. Hood, Texas as 35th Armor . . . presently serving with the Division in Bavaria, Germany.

37th TANK BATTALION

When the 4th Armored Division was activated in April 15, 1941, the 7th Armored Regiment was already one of the units assigned to the Division. On May 8th, 1941 it was redesignated as the 37th Armored Regiment. In September 1943 the division was reorganized into a "light" armored division and the 37th became the 37th Tank Bn.... with both light and medium tanks.

CAMPAIGNS: Normandy, Northern France, Ardennes-Alsace, Rhineland, Central Europe.

DECORATIONS: Distinguished Unit Citation: "ARDENNES," 22 Dec. 1944, 27 March 1945. WD GO 54-45.
French Fourragere: "NORMANDY" and "MOSELLE RIVER" 27 July, 11 Aug. '44 and 12-29 Sept. '44 DA GO 43-50.
French Croix de Guerre w/Palm for Normandy and Moselle River.

MOTTO: "Courage Conquers"

DESCRIPTION: The coat of arms was approved 1 June 1942. The shield is green and white, the colors of the Armored Forces of W.W. II. The wyvern (a representation of a chimerical animal imagined as a winged dragon) depicts the deadliness of the tank. A crest above the shield was approved August 6, 1965 and stands for the three outstanding combat achievements in W W. II for which the unit was awarded streamers embroidered "Ardennes," "Normandy," and "Moselle River." It also represents the unit's spearheading the 4th Armored Division into Bastogne on 26 Dec. 1944.

COMMANDERS IN COMBAT: Lt. Col. Creighton W. Abrams, Maj. Wm. L. Hunter, Maj. Edward Bautz, Jr., Capt. Wm. A. Dwight.

COMMANDERS IN OCCUPATION: Lt. Col. Leslie R. Wilcox.

The 37th Tank Bn. was redesignated as the 37th Constabulary Sqdn. in occupation and redesignated back to the 37th Tank Bn. in Nov. 1953, and further redesignated 37th Armor, January 28, 1958. The unit is presently serving with the 4th Armored Division in Bavaria, Germany.

174

10th ARMORED INFANTRY BATTALION

When the 4th Armored Division became a "light" Armored Division on September 10, 1943, the 2nd Battalion, 51st Armored Infantry Battalion was redesignated 10th Armored Infantry Battalion, organic element of the 4th Armored Division. Converted and redesignated 10th Constabulary Squadron, relieved from assignment to the 4th Armored Division and assigned to 14th Constabulary Regiment May 1, 1946. Converted and redesignated 10th Armored Infantry Battalion, relieved from assignment to 14th Constabulary Regiment and assigned to 4th Armored Division, and inactivated in Germany December 20, 1948. Redesignated 510th Armored Infantry Battalion February 25, 1953.

CAMPAIGNS: Normandy, Northern France, Ardennes-Alsace, Rhineland, Central Europe.

DECORATIONS: Distinguished Unit Citation: "ARDENNES" 22 Dec. 1944, 27 March 1945. WD GO 54-55.
French Fourragere: "NORMANDY" and "MOSELLE RIVER" 27 July, 11 Aug. '44 and 12-29 Sept. '44 DA GO 43-50.
French Croix de Guerre w/Palm (Fourragere) DA GO 43-50, '39-'45.

MOTTO: "Only The Best."

DESCRIPTION OF SHIELD: The shield is blue for Infantry. Service of the parent regiment (51st Infantry) in World War I is shown by the bend from the coat of arms of Alsace. Descent from the 2nd Battalion, 51st Armored Infantry Regiment, is shown by the border gyronny gold and blue.

COMMANDERS IN COMBAT: Lt. Col. Graham Kirkpatrick, Lt. Col. Arthur L. West, Lt. Col. Harold Cohen.

COMMANDER IN OCCUPATION: Major Fred B. Hammond, Jr.

51st ARMORED INFANTRY BATTALION

LINEAGE: Parent unit constituted 15 May 1917 as 51st Inf. Regt. Organized 22 May 1917, at Chickamauga Park, Ga., from personnel of 11th Inf. Regt. Assigned to 6th Div. 16 Nov. 1917. Inactivated 22 Sept. 1921 at Camp Grant, Ill. with 53rd Inf. Regt. made active associate 17 July 1921. Relieved from assignment to 6th Div. and assigned to 9th Div. 15 Aug. 1927. Relieved from assignment to 6th Div. 16 Dec. 1940. Assigned to 4th Armd. Div. 13 Jan. 1941. Activated 15 April 1941 at Pine Camp, N.Y. Redesignated 51st Armd. Inf. Regt. 1 Jan. 1942. Regiment broken up and redesignated 10 Sept. 1943 as follows: Regiment (less 1st and 2nd Bns.) as 51st Armd. Inf. Bn.; (1st Bn. as 53rd Armd. Inf. Bn.; 2nd Bn. as 10th Armd. Inf. Bn.)

51st Armd. Inf. Bn. converted and redesignated 51st Constabulary Sqdn., relieved from assignment to 4th Armd. Div. and assigned to 11th Constabulary Regt., 1 May 1946. Converted and redesignated 51st Armd. Inf. Bn., relieved from assignment to 11th Constabulary Regt. and assigned to 4th Armd. Div. on 10 May 1971, was absorbed into the 1st Armd. Div. now serving in Germany . . . in the 7th Army.

CAMPAIGNS: W.W. I: Alsace, Meuse-Argonne. W.W. II: Normandy, Northern France, Ardennes-Alsace, Rhineland, Central Europe.

DECORATIONS: Distinguished Unit Citation for ARDENNES French Croix de Guerre w/Palm for NORMANDY and MOSELLE RIVER. French Fourragerre.

MOTTO: "I Serve"

DESCRIPTION: *Shield:* Azure, a bend or. *Crest:* On a wreath of the colors or and azure a ragged tree trunk eradicated proper. A shield is blue for Infantry, with the bend taken from the coat of arms of Alsace. Coat of arms originally approved on 24 January 1930.

COMMANDERS IN COMBAT: Lt. Col. Alfred A. Maybach, Maj. Harry Van Arnam, Lt. Col. Dan C. Alanis.

COMMANDER IN OCCUPATION: Lt. Col. Warren B. Haskell.

53rd ARMORED INFANTRY BATTALION

LINEAGE: On September 10, 1943, when the 4th Armored Division was reorganized into a "light" division, the 1st Battalion, 51st Armored Infantry Regiment was redesignated the 53rd Armored Infantry Battalion. Converted and redesignated 53rd Constabulary Squadron, relieved from assignment to 4th Armored Division and assigned to 6th Constabulary Regiment, 1 May 1946. Relieved from assignment to 6th Constabulary Regiment and assigned to U.S. Constabulary 16 November 1948. Converted and redesignated 53rd Armored Infantry Battalion, inactivated, relieved from assignment to U.S. Constabulary and assigned to 4th Armored Division, 20 May 1949. Redesignated 553rd Armored Infantry Battalion 25 February 1953.

CAMPAIGNS: Normandy, Northern France, Rhineland, Ardennes-Alsace, Central Europe.

DECORATIONS: Distinguished Unit Citation for ARDENNES French Croix de Guerre w/Palm for NORMANDY and MOSELLE RIVER. French Fourragerre.

MOTTO: "Ever Onward"

DESCRIPTION: Shield. The shield of the 51st Infantry Regiment is used witin the border to show descent of the 53rd Armored Infantry Battalion from the 1st Battalion of that regiment. The shield is blue for Infantry. Service of the parent regiment in W.W. I is shown by the bend from the coat of arms of Alsace.

COMMANDER IN COMBAT: Lt. Col. George L. Jaques.

COMMANDER IN OCCUPATION: Lt. Col. Clarence O. Brunner.

24th ARMORED ENGINEER BATTALION

The 24th Armored Engineer Battalion was constituted 15 August 1917 as the 24th Engineers (Supply & Shop). Organized November 1917 as Co's F, D, & E, 26th Engineers transferred to the 24th Engineers in November; Co. F organized as Co. F, 25th Engineers, transferred to 24th Engineers in November; remainder of regiment organized new. Demobilized 3 June 1919 at Camp Jackson, So. Carolina. Reconstituted and consolidated 3 April 1931 with the 24 Engrs. (General Service). Redesignated 16 Dec. 1940 as 24th Engineer Battalion (Armored). Activated 15 April 1941 at Pine Camp, N.Y. as an element of the 4th Armored Division. Redesignated 5 January 1942 as 24th Armored Engineer Bn. (Co. D withdrawn from 4th Armored Division 10 Sept. 1943, disbanded 10 Nov. 1943; Co. E redesignated 988th Treadway Bridge Co., 10 Sept. 1943. Inactivated 21 April 1946 at Camp Kilmer, N.J. Activated 15 June 1954 at Ft. Hood, Texas. Redesignated 1 April 1957 as 24th Engineer Battalion.

CAMPAIGNS: World War I: St. Mihiel, Meuse-Argonne. World War II: Normandy, No. France, Rhineland, Ardennes-Alsace, Central Europe.

DECORATIONS: Distinguished Unit Citation for ARDENNES French Croix de Guerre (w/Palm) for NORMANDY and MOSELLE RIVER. Fourragere, French Croix de Guerre.

MOTTO: None

SYMBOLISM: The coat of arms was originally approved for the 24th Regiment Engineers 26 June 1931. The shield is red with the charge in silver, the colors of the Engineer Corps. The eagle's head is taken from one of the supporters of the coat of arms of St. Mihiel where the 24th Regiment Engrs. saw action in W.W. I. The eagle's head is gorged with a collar sable charged with a Lorraine cross of the second.

COMMANDERS IN COMBAT: Lt. Col. Louis E. Roth, Maj. Alonzo A. Balcom, Lt. Col. Wm. L. Nungesser, Maj. Donald W. Hatch.

COMMANDER IN OCCUPATION: Lt. Col. Sears Y. Coker.

22nd ARMORED FIELD ARTILLERY BATTALION

LINEAGE: Headquarters, Headquarters Detachment and Combat Trains, Batteries A and B, organized 1918 as the Separate Battalion Mountain Artillery with nucleus from the Fourth Field Artillery; redesignated the First Battalion, 22nd Field Artillery, 1921. Made inactive Sept. 15, 1921. Second and third Battalions authorized on the inactive list August 16, 1921. Served with the 4th Armored Division from the Division's activation, April 15, 1941 to the Division's 22nd Armd. Field activation, May 10, 1971.

CAMPAIGNS: Normandy, Northern France, Rhineland, Ardennes-Alsace, and Central Europe.

DECORATIONS: Distinguished Unit Citation for ARDENNES French Croix de Guerre w/Palm for NORMANDY and MOSELLE RIVER. Fr. Fourragerre.

MOTTO: "Labore et Honore" (With Industry and Honor.)

SYMBOLISM: The shield is red for Artillery. The transfer of personnel from the 4th Field Artillery when the 22nd Field Artillery was organized (10 July 1918) is indicated by the canton, which is the shield of the 4th Field Artillery coat of arms. (The 4th Field Artillery was originally a regiment of mountain artillery and the bend sinister is an allusion to the hybrid mule with which it was equipped.) The crest is taken from the arms of the Panama Canal, indicating the place the 22nd Field Artillery was organized.

COMMANDER IN COMBAT: Lt. Col. Arthur C. Peterson. (Same in occupation.)

66th ARMORED FIELD ARTILLERY BATTALION

The 66th Field Artillery constituted 16 December 1940 in the Regular Army, and assigned to the 4th Armored Division. Activated 15 April 1941 at Pine Camp, New York. Reorganized and redesignated 1 January 1942 as 66th Armored Field Artillery Battalion. Served with the 4th Armored Division during all its training, combat and occupation years. Assigned 25 January 1953 to the 4th Armored Division; activated 15 June 1954 at Fort Hood, Texas; inactivated 1 April 1957 at Ft. Hood, Texas, and concurrently, relieved from assignment to the 4th Armored Division. Hqs/Hqs Btry, 55th Field Arty Group, 55th Field Arty Bn., 50th Field Arty Bn. (less Hqs/Hqs Btry) and 66th Armored Field Bn consolidated, reorganized and redesignated 31 July 1959 as 55th Artillery, a parent regiment under the Combat Arms Regimental System.

CAMPAIGNS: Normandy, Northern France, Ardennes-Alsace, Rhineland, Central Europe.

DECORATIONS: Distinguished Unit Citation: ARDENNES. French Croix de Guerre w/Palm for NORMANDY and MOSELLE RIVER. French Fourragerre.

MOTTO: "Fire"

SYMBOLISM: The red of the shield is representative of Artillery and the arrangement of the shells produces the numerical designation of the organization.

COMMANDERS IN COMBAT: Lt. Col. Neil M. Wallace (KIA), Lt. Col. F. W. Hasselback.

COMMANDER IN OCCUPATION: Lt. Col. Frederick W. Hasselback.

We are aware that the 66th Field Artillery saw action during W.W. I in the campaigns of Aisne-Marne, Champagne, Oisene-Aisne, and Meuse-Argonne. Other than that we have no information.

94th ARMORED FIELD ARTILLERY BATTALION

The 94th Field Artillery constituted 1 October 1933 in the Regular Army... redesignated 1 January 1942 as 94th Armored Field Artillery Battalion. Activated 6 January 1942 at Pine Camp, N.Y., as an element of the 4th Armored Division. Converted, reorganized and redesignated 1 May 1946 as 94th Constabulary Squadron. Concurrently, relieved from assignment to the 4th Armored Division and assigned to the 11th Constabulary Regiment. Converted reorganized and redesignated 6 January 1948 as 94th Field Artillery Bn. and relieved from assignment to the 11th Constabulary Regiment. Inactivated 20 May 1949 in Germany. Concurrently, redesignated 94th Armored Field Artillery Bn. and assigned to the 4th Armored Division. Activated 15 June 1954 at Fort Hood, Texas. Inactivated 1 April 1957 at Fort Hood, Texas, and relieved from assignment to the 4th Armored Division. Concurrently, Battalion redesignated 94th Artillery, a parent regiment under the Combat Arms Regiment System.

CAMPAIGNS: Normandy, Northern France, Rhineland, Ardennes-Alsace, Central Europe.

DECORATIONS: Distinguished Unit Citation: ARDENNES. French Croix de Guerre w/Palm: NORMANDY and MOSELLE RIVER. French Fourragere.

MOTTO: "Flexible"

SYMBOLISM: The shield is divided scarlet and yellow; scarlet being the Artillery color and yellow the color of Artillery guidon markings. The charge is known as a guisarme, a weapon used in ancient times to reach the enemy behind the defense. It symbolizes the operations of the organization.

COMMANDERS IN COMBAT: Lt. Col. Alexander Graham, Lt. Col. Lloyd W. Powers, Lt. Col. Robert M. Parker, Jr.

COMMANDER IN OCCUPATION: Lt. Col. Robert M. Parker, Jr.

181

25th CAVALRY RECONNAISSANCE
SQUADRON, MECHANIZED

The 4th Reconnaissance Battalion (Armored) constituted January 13 1941 in the Regular Army and assigned to the 4th Armored Division. Activated 15 April 1941 at Pine Camp, N.Y. On May 8, 1941 it was redesignated as 84th Reconnaissance Battalion (Armored). On Jan. 1, 1942 redesignated as 84th Armored Reconnaissance Battalion. In September 1943 when the 4th Armored was reorganized into a "light" division, the 84th was converted and redesignated as 25th Cavalry Reconnaissance Squadron, Mechanized. Reconnaissance Co. of the 35th Armored Regiment became Troop D, while Reconnaissance Co. of the 37th Armored Regiment became Troop E.

CAMPAIGNS: Normandy, Northern France, Ardennes-Alsace, Rhineland, Central Europe.

DECORATIONS: Distinguished Unit Citation: ARDENNES, 22 Dec. 1944, 27 March 1945. WD GO 54-55.
French Fourragere: NORMANDY and MOSELLE RIVER, 27 July, 11 Aug. '44 and 12-29 Sept. '44 DA GO 43-50.
French Croix de Guerre w/Palm (Fourragere) DA GO 43-50 '39-'45.

MOTTO: "Information."

DESCRIPTION OF SHIELD: Vert, an octopus argent, the arm in dexter chief grasping a pine cone proper.

COMMANDERS IN COMBAT: Lt. Col. Leslie D. Goodall.

COMMANDERS IN OCCUPATION: Captain Lawrence J. Zielinski.

On May 1, 1946 converted and redesignated as 25th Constabulary Squadron; relieved from assignment to 4th Armored Division. Converted and redesignated Dec. 20, 1948 as 25th Reconnaissance Battalion; concurrently, inactivated. Assigned to 4th Armored Division Feb. 25, 1953. Activated June 15, 1954 at Ft. Hood, Tex. Hdqtrs. and Service Co's. consolidated into 50th Cavalry April 1, 1957. Companies A, B, & C redesignated as Troops. Co. D inactivated April 1, 1957; subsequently redesignated an element of 35th Armor.

182

126th ARMORED ORDNANCE MAINTENANCE BATTALION

LINEAGE: At the activation of the 4th Armd. Div. on April 15, 1941 at Pine Camp, N.Y., the 19th Ordnance Bn. of the 1st Armd. Div. from Ft. Knox, Ky. was the cadre for what was to become the 20th Ordnance Bn. on May 1941, Pine Camp, N.Y. On Jan. 13, 1941, it was designated Maintenance Bn., 4th Armd. Div. and activated Jan. 5, 1942 ... reorganized and redesignated Sept. 10, 1943 as 126th Ordnance Maintenance Bn ... redesignated April 18, 1945 as 126th *Armored* Ordnance Maintenance Bn. Inactivated April 23, 1946 at Camp Kilmer, N.J. Redesignated May 28, 1954 as 126th Armored Ordnance Bn., and activated June 15, 1954 at Ft. Hood, Texas with 4th Armd. Div. Reorganized and redesignated April 1, 1957 as 126th Ord. Bn. (Hq & Hqs Co.) and Co. A consolidated and redesignated Hq and Co. A (Main Support) concurrently Co. D constituted and activated. Reorganized and redesignated 6 May 1963 as 126th Maintenance Bn. Served with 4th Armd. Div. in the 7th Army in Germany until it was inactivated 10 May 1971.

DECORATIONS: Distinguished Unit Citation: ARDENNES. French Croix de Guerre (w/Palm) for NORMANDY and MOSELLE RIVER. Fourragere: French Croix de Guerre.

CAMPAIGNS: Northern France, Normandy, Rhineland, Ardennes-Alsace, Central Europe.

MOTTO: "Uniqi'e Wowas'ak'e Unu'ha'pi" (We Maintain Strength).

SYMBOLISM: Insignia approved 10 Oct. 1942. The split fields of green and scarlet illustrate the versatility and two-fold job of the Maintenance Bn. in the Armored Force and the fusion into one unit. The silver broken gear indicates the responsibilities of the unit in regard to all vehicles, and the darker silver cannon represents the armament sections, while both show the formidable strength of the organization. The motto is apparent in American Indian language (Sioux tribe of Dakota) meaning the battalion is the heartbeat of the Armored Division, maintaining as nearly its total strength as possible to allow it to continue to fight. Strength is within the battalion itself, as applied to its own vehicles, personnel, and fire power.

COMMANDER IN COMBAT: Lt. Col. Richard B. Euller.

COMMANDER IN OCCUPATION: Major Frank T. Henry.

46th ARMORED MEDICAL BATTALION

At the activation of the 4th Armored Division on April 15, 1941 at Pine Camp, N.Y., the 47th Medical Battalion of the 1st Armd. Division from Ft. Knox, Ky., was the cadre for what was to become the 46th Medical Bn. On Jan. 1, 1942, the battalion was redesignated as the 46th *Armored* Medical Battalion.

CAMPAIGNS: Normandy, Northern France, Ardennes-Alsace, Rhineland, Central Europe.

DECORATIONS: Distinguished Unit Citation: ARDENNES. French Croix de Guerre with Palm for NORMANDY and MOSELLE RIVER. Fourragere: French Croix de Guerre.

MOTTO: "Ut Iterum Servias." (That You May Serve Again)

SYMBOLISM: The coat of arms was approved February 12, 1942. The shield is in the colors of the Medical Corps. The cross symbolizes the nature of the battalion and the pine tree the location at which it was made active, Pine Camp, New York.

Inactivated 24 April 1946 at Camp Kilmer, N.J.

Activated 15 June 1954 at Fort Hood, Texas—an organic element of the 4th Armored Division—serving in the 7th Army in Germany.

Inactivated 10 May 1971 in Germany.

COMMANDER IN COMBAT: Lt. Col. Robert E. Mailliard.

COMMANDER IN OCCUPATION: Major George V. Potter.

The combat men of the 4th Armored Division remember well and "salute" the 46th Armored Medical Battalion...remembering how the cries of the wounded sounding, "Medic!!" were answered quickly and bravely by the men carrying no weapons but only the tools of the first aid kit.

185

144th ARMORED SIGNAL COMPANY

LINEAGE: At the activation of the 4th Armd. Div. on April 15, 1941 at Pine Camp, N.Y., the 47th Signal Co. of the 1st Armd. Div. from Ft. Knox, Ky., was the cadre for what was to become the 144th Signal Co. The new Signal Co. at Pine Camp was first known as the 49th Signal Co. On Jan. 5, 1942 when the Armored Divisions underwent reorganization, the 144th Armored Signal Co. came into being.

CAMPAIGNS: Normandy, Northern France, Rhineland, Ardennes-Alsace, Central Europe.

DECORATIONS: Distinguished Unit Citation: ARDENNES. French Croix de Guerre (w/Palm) for NORMANDY and MOSELLE RIVER. Fourragere, French Croix de Guerre.

MOTTO: "Vox Vincentis." (Voice of the Victorious).

SYMBOLISM: The coat of arms was approved 4 April 1958. Orange and white are the colors for the Signal Corps. The four white diagonal bands suggest lines of communication and represent the unit's four W.W. II decorations. The fleur-de-lis, from the historic French coat of arms, indicates that the battalion has been decorated by the French Govt. The lion, a device from the Arms of Normandy, is placed in the position of honor on the upper portion of the shield in commemoration of the unit's action against the enemy during the Battle of Normandy.

Inactivated 24 April 1946 at Camp Kilmer, N.J. Activated 15 June 1954 at Ft. Hood, Texas, as organic element of 4th Armored Division. Redesignated and reorganized 1 April 1957 as Hqs. and Hqs. Co. 144th Signal Bn.; organic elements concurrently constituted and activated at Ft. Hood, Texas. Inactivated 10 May 1971 in Germany.

COMMANDER IN COMBAT: Capt. Lucien E. Trosclair.

COMMANDER IN OCCUPATION: Capt. John G. Moses.

COMBAT COMMAND A

COMBAT COMMAND A: Following the entrance of the 4th Armored Division in W.W. II, Combat Command A led the way in cutting off the Brittany Peninsula in August 1944. Upon completion of the mission, the command moved 80 miles in seven hours to arrive in Nantes where they stormed the city and subdued all resistance. This, in addition to the battle of Orleans, was the first of many daring exploits made by CC A during the European campaign.

An SS Colonel captured by CC A emphasized the reputation of this command when he remarked in wonder at the ability of our army ". . . to achieve such a spurt of advance, which in many instances caught us completely unprepared."

Perhaps one of the highlights of the command's combat record is the heroic part played in the bitter and bloody fighting at Bastogne nearly five months later.

Reflecting the leading role held during the war by CC A, nearly 9000 casualties were inflicted upon the enemy by units of this command.

Upon the reactivation of the division on 15 June 1954, CC A played a large role in the keeping of peace in Germany and participated in German-American Relationship when it arrived in Germany in December 1957 and added greatly in the good will program of the famed 4th Armored Division.

CAMPAIGNS: Normandy, Northern France, Ardennes-Alsace, Rhineland, Central Europe.

DECORATIONS: Distinguished Unit Citation for action during the period 22 Dec. 1944 to 27 Mar. 1945. Streamer embroidered BASTOGNE. Fr. Cr. de Guerre w/Palm for NORMANDY and MOSELLE RIVER.

COMMANDERS: Maj. Gen. Roderick R. Allen (25 April 42-31 Oct. 43); Gen. Bruce C. Clarke (1 Nov. 43-31 Oct. 44); Gen. Creighton W. Abrams, Jr. (1 Nov. 44-18 Nov. 44); Col. Wm. P. Withers (19 Nov. 44-3 Dec. 44); Maj. Gen. Herbert L. Earnest (4 Dec. 44-31 Dec. 44); Col. Hayden A. Sears (25 Jan. 45-9 Sept. 45); Brig. Gen. John B. Sullivan (6 Oct. 45-31 Mar. 46).

COMBAT COMMAND B: After its move to England in Jan. '44, CC B went into the secret concentration area of the Division in Normandy in July '44. CC B made its first offensive thrust south of Carentan, 28 July '44, drove through the village of Periers and took the first French city to fall to the Division, Coutances. In the ensuing weeks, CC B led a 54 mile drive to Redon and then followed Pont Scorff on the outskirts of the huge German U boat base at Lorient. Then a 264 mile trek in 34 hrs. to Prensy, south of Vendome followed by a 50 mile run north to fill a gap at La Loupe. In Sept. '44 CC B and CC A alternately spearheaded the Division's 750 mile right hook across the heart of France. One of the most dramatic missions CC B fulfilled was a 151 mile dash in 19 hrs. to new positions south of the German penetration in the Belgian Ardennes. With CC B at the fore, the 4th Armd. Div. broke through the German perimeter in 4 days and "liberated" elements of the 101st Airborne Div. which had been surrounded at Bastogne. On 8 Mar. '44, Col. C. W. Abrams then battalion commander of our 37th Tank Bn. succeeded Gen. Dager as C.O. of CC B and continued its mobile thrusts into the heart of Germany and then pushed south through Bavaria and deep into Czechoslavakia enroute to Prague as the war ended 5/9/45.

The initial area of German occupation assigned to the 4th Armd. was southeast of Nurnberg, astride the Danube. CC B now under Col. W. A. Bixby was in the Landshut area.

When the Division first attacked on 28 July 1944, that day began the enfolding of one of the classic examples of mobile warfare, an example that serves today to identify the 4th Armored Division as the criterion for the measurement of achievements of modern American fighting units.

In April 1946 the 4th Armored Division was absorbed in the U.S. Constabulary and the Division was inactivated. The 4th Armored was re-activated in June 1954 at Fort Hood, Texas and moved to Germany in Nov. 1957. CC B was stationed in Erlangen and controlled all Division units stationed in the Greater Nurnberg area . . . it had but one mission: To be ready to fight! The 4th Armored Division was inactivated on 10 May 1971 . . . and sorely missed by many who served under her.

CAMPAIGNS: Normandy, Northern France, Ardennes-Alsace, Rhineland, Central Europe.

DECORATIONS: Distinguished Unit Citation for action during the period 22 Dec. 1944 to 27 Mar. 1945. Streamer embroidered BASTOGNE. Fr. Croix de Guerre w/Palm for NORMANDY and MOSELLE RIVER.

COMMANDERS IN COMBAT: Brig. Gen. (later Maj. Gen.) Holmes E. Dager; Col. (later Gen.-Chief of Staff) Creighton W. Abrams.

APPENDIX II

ATTACHED UNITS IN COMBAT

704th TANK DESTROYER BATTALION

489th ANTI-AIRCRAFT ARTILLERY (AW)
BATTALION (SP)

3804th QUARTERMASTER TRUCK COMPANY

444th QUARTERMASTER TRUCK COMPANY

995th ENGINEER TREADWAY BRIDGE COMPANY

696th ARMORED FIELD ARTILLERY BATTALION

1st PLATOON 16th FIELD HOSPITAL

456th AMBULANCE COMPANY

5th DETACHMENT, 166th SIGNAL PHOTO COMPANY

COUNTERINTELLIGENCE CORPS DETACHMENT No. 504

INTERROGATION OF PRISONERS OF WAR TEAMS
No. 56 and 61

ORDER OF BATTLE TEAM No. 24

AIR SUPPORT PARTY No. 2, XIX TACTICAL
AIR COMMAND

PHOTO INTELLIGENCE TEAM No. 56

ADVANCE SECTION COMMUNICATIONS ZONE,
PROSTHETIC TEAM No. 4

704th TANK DESTROYER BATTALION

The 704th Tank Destroyer Battalion was constituted December 3, 1941. It was activated with a nucleus from "D" Battery, 22nd Armored Field Artillery Battalion on December 15, 1941, at Pine Camp, N.Y. and was virtually a part of the 4th Armored Division.

CAMPAIGNS: Normandy, Northern France, Ardennes-Alsace, Rhineland, Central Europe.

DECORATIONS: Distinguished Unit Citation for action during the period 22 December 1944 to 27 March 1945. Streamer embroidered BASTOGNE.

MOTTO: "Victory Not Glory"

SYMBOLISM: Yellow and green are the colors used for Armor. Black and yellow are the historic Tank Destroyer colors. The unit's constitution and service as a Tank Destroyer unit is therefore depicted by the jagged triangular device charged with an acorn to commemorate the battalion's valiant and distinguished defense of Bastogne. The five bars symbolize the organization's five World War II European campaign honors.

Inactivated 25 October 1945 at Camp Shanks, N.Y. Converted and redesignated 27 August 1947 as 329th Mechanized Cavalry Reconnaissance Sqdn and allotted to the Organized Reserves. Activated 24 September 1947 at Lansing, Michigan. Converted and redesignated 329th Heavy Tank Ban., 22 March 1949 and reorganized 6 June 1950 as 329th Tank Bn. Inactivated 4 Dec. 1950 at Lansing, Mich. Withdrawn from the Organized Reserve Corps, allotted to the Regular Army, and redesignated as 704th Tank Destroyer Bn., 30 July 1951. Redesignated 704th Tank Bn. and assigned to 4th Armored Division 25 Feb. 1953. Activated 15 June 1954 at Ft. Hood, Texas. Inactivated 1 April 1957 at Ft. Hood, Texas.

COMMANDERS IN COMBAT: Lt. Col. Delk M. Oden, Lt. Col. Bill A. Bailey, Lt. Col. Henry P. Heid, Jr., Major Dan C. Alanis, Maj. Chas. I. Kimsey, Lt. Col. James W. Bidwell.

489th ANTI-AIRCRAFT ARTILLERY (AW)
BATTALION (SP)

The 489th Antiaircraft Artillery Automatic Weapons Battalion (SP) was activated February 10, 1943 at Ft. Bliss, Texas. In December of 1943 they participated in the Louisiana Maneuvers and in March 1944 they landed in England. The Battalion trained in Wrexham, Wales. Until they joined the Third U.S. Army and the 4th Armored Division on July 13 in Normandy, they provided antiaircraft protection for English airfields.

CAMPAIGNS: Normandy, Northern France, Ardennes-Alsace, Rhineland, Central Europe.

DECORATIONS: Distinguished Unit Citation for action during the period 22 December 1944 to 27 March 1945. Streamer embroidered BASTOGNE. Fr. Croix de Guerre.

MOTTO: "Duty, Honor, Above All."

SYMBOLISM: The coat of arms was approved 5 June 1953. The shield is in the colors of Artillery . . . Red. The partition line represents the horizon. The mullets, symbolizing flak bursts, form a "box of flak": One burst for each of the organization's campaigns in Europe during W.W. II. The unit was disbanded (less Battery A) in 1959. Battery A, 489th AAA Battalion was redesignated Battery E (AD), 356th Regiment (AIT), formerly the 356th Infantry Regiment.

The 489th destroyed their first enemy plane...an ME 109... on July 19, 1944, and had a grand total destroyed by April 30, 1945 of 128½ and 41 probables. Maj. Gen. John S. Wood, commander of the 4th Armored Division, on 15 October 1944 commended the officers and men of the Battalion for their outstanding performances, and said: "So effective was their fire that this battalion set the highest record for accuracy in the destruction of enemy aircraft in the entire army."

COMMANDER IN ACTIVATION AND COMBAT: Lt. Col. Allen M. Murphy.

995th ENGINEER TREADWAY BRIDGE COMPANY

The 995th Engineer Treadway Bridge Co. was cadred from Co. E. 56th Armored Engineers Battalion, 11th Armored Division . . . at Camp Polk, La. In September 1943, they set forth to Camp Barkeley, Texas to become the 995th . . . training, maneuvers, etc. followed.

The 995th left Camp Barkeley at the end of January 1944 arriving at Camp Kilmer, N.J. their Port of Embarkation. Leaving the U.S. in February 1944, they landed in Liverpool, England and boarded the trains for Southern England, Ross-on-Rye.

On June 24th, 1944, the 995th landed in Utah Beach, Vindefontaine, Pont L'Abbe. The 995th were among the first of their type bridge company to land in France. They soon became attached to the Third Army and Gen. George S. Patton's favorite Division . . . the 4th Armored Division! They then started playing that game, "one more river to cross!" They raced to Rennes with the 4th, they raced to Sens with the 4th, to Nancy, to Arracourt, the Ardennes and the "Bulge" . . . they crossed the Marne, the Moselle, the Inn, the Isar, the Seine, the Main, the Danube and many smaller rivers. Theirs was the first Third Army bridge across the Rhine.

They built everything they were asked to build and they built themselves a name. They were *The* bridge company of *The* great 4th Armored Division of *The* great Third Army! They laid nearly 3,000 feet of bridge in France, nearly 1,000 in Luxembourg, nearly 4,000 feet in Germany and Austria, and several hundred in Belgium . . . a grand total of 7,766 feet made up of 121 bridges ranging from 12 feet to 972 feet.

CAMPAIGNS: Normandy, Northern France, Ardennes-Alsace, Rhineland, Central Europe.

DECORATIONS: Distinguished Unit Citation and numerous letters of commendation.

Though theirs was comparatively a small Company, their members received 23 Bronze Star Medals, 17 Purple Hearts and a number more posthumously.

APPENDIX III

THE COMMANDERS IN COMBAT

4th Armored Division
  Major General John S. Wood
  Major General Hugh J. Gaffey
  Major General William M. Hoge

Combat Command B
  Brigadier General Holmes E. Dager
  Colonel Creighton W. Abrams

Combat Command A
  Colonel Bruce C. Clarke
  Lieutenant Colonel Creighton W. Abrams
  Colonel William P. Withers
  Brigadier General Herbert L. Earnest
  Colonel Hayden A. Sears

Division Artillery
  Colonel Ernest A. Bixby
  Colonel Alexander Graham
  Lieutenant Colonel Neil M. Wallace

Reserve Command
  Colonel Louis J. Storck*
  Colonel Walter A. Bigby
  Colonel Wendell Blanchard

Division Trains
  Colonel David A. Watt Jr.
  Colonel Wendell Blanchard

10th Armored Infantry Battalion
  Lieutenant Colonel Graham Kirkpatrick**
  Lieutenant Colonel Arthur L. West**
  Lieutenant Colonel Harold Cohen

51st Armored Infantry Battalion
 Lieutenant Colonel Alfred A. Maybach*
 Major Harry R. Van Arnam**
 Lieutenant Colonel Dan C. Alanis

53rd Armored Infantry Battalion
 Lieutenant Colonel George L. Jaques

8th Tank Battalion
 Lieutenant Colonel Edgar T. Conley Jr.
 Lieutenant Colonel Henry P. Heid Jr.
 Major Thomas G. Churchill
 Lieutenant Colonel Albin F. Irzyk

35th Tank Battalion
 Lieutenant Colonel Bill A. Bailey
 Lieutenant Colonel Delk M. Oden

37th Tank Battalion
 Lieutenant Colonel Creighton W. Abrams
 Major William L. Hunter**
 Major Edward Bautz Jr.
 Captain William A. Dwight

25th Cavalry Reconnaissance Squadron, Mechanized
 Lieutenant Colonel Leslie D. Goodall

22nd Armored Field Artillery Battalion
 Lieutenant Colonel Arthur C. Peterson

6th Armored Field Artillery Battalion
 Lieutenant Colonel Neil M. Wallace**
 Lieutenant Colonel F. W. Hasselback

94th Armored Field Artillery Battalion
 Lieutenant Colonel Alexander Graham
 Lieutenant Colonel Lloyd W. Powers
 Lieutenant Colonel Robert M. Parker Jr.

24th Armored Engineer Battalion
Lieutenant Colonel Louis E. Roth
Major Alonzo A. Balcom Jr.
Lieutenant Colonel William L. Nungesser**
Major Donald W. Hatch

126th Armored Ordnance Maintenance Battalion
Lieutenant Colonel Richard B. Euller

704th Tank Destroyer Battalion
Lieutenant Colonel Delk M. Oden
Lieutenant Colonel Bill A. Bailey*
Lieutenant Colonel Henry P. Heid Jr.
Major Dan C. Alanis
Major Charles I. Kimsey
Lieutenant Colonel James W. Bidwell

489th Anti Aircraft Artillery (AW) Battalion (SP)
Lieutenant Colonel Allen M. Murphy

46th Armored Medical Battalion
Lieutenant Colonel Robert E. Mailliard

144th Armored Signal Company
Captain Lucien E. Trosclair

Headquarters Company, Combat Command A
Captain Ottis Strong
Captain Alfred Owens

Headquarters Company, Combat Command B
Captain Richard R. Irving

Headquarters Battery, Division Artillery
Captain Clarence E. Visscher

Headquarters Company, 4th Armored Division
Captain Nelson D. Warwick

Headquarters Company, Division Trains
Captain La Rue McCleary

*killed in action
**relinquished command because of wounds received in action

APPENDIX IV

THE DIVISION STAFF IN COMBAT

Assistant Division Commander
    Brigadier General William L. Roberts

Chief of Staff
    Colonel Walter A. Bigby
    Lieutenant Colonel David A. Watt Jr.
    Colonel Ernest A. Bixby

G-1
    Lieutenant Colonel Robert M. Connolly
    Lieutenant Colonel John H. Himelick

G-2
    Lieutenant Colonel Harry E. Brown

G-3
    Lieutenant Colonel John B. Sullivan

G-4
    Lieutenant Colonel Herbert F. Krucker
    Lieutenant Colonel Bernard C. Knestrick

G-5
    Lieutenant Colonel James Van Wagenen

Adjutant General
    Lieutenant Colonel John H. Himelick
    Lieutenant Colonel Robert M. Connolly

Division Surgeon
    Lieutenant Colonel Morris Abrams

Division Chaplain
    Lieutenant Colonel Emmet P. Crane

Division Signal Officer
Lieutenant Colonel Otto T. Saar

Division Quartermaster
Lieutenant Colonel Bernard C. Knestrick
Lieutenant Colonel Gerald E. Miller

Division Finance Officer
Lieutenant Colonel Geroge L. Eatman

Division Chemical Warfare Officer
Lieutenant Colonel Lawrence F. Dorato

Judge Advocate General
Lieutenant Colonel Chester D. Silvers

Division Finance Officer
Lieutenant Colonel George L. Eatman

Inspector General
Lieutenant Colonel Clarence O. Brunner

Provost Marshal
Major John R. Kerr

Special Service Officer
Major John W. Gander

Headquarters Commandant
Major George N. Calvert

Division Public Relations Officer
First Lieutenant Kenneth A. Koyen

Division Bandmaster
Chief Warrant Officer Richard E. Velasco